Economic and Financial Aspects of Development - National and International

Economic and Financial Aspects of Development - National and International

M Hedayetul Haque

ISBN: 1514170922
ISBN 13: 9781514170922

Preface

The present work 'Economic and Financial Aspects of Development – National and International' is a compilation of various articles that I wrote in the past few years after my retirement from Government service and completion of an assignment abroad under an international organization abroad. Almost all of these articles were published in various newspapers in Bangladesh.

The idea behind this compilation is intended to provide an analytical background and understanding to the academicians and the primary researchers on the economic and financial policies of the Government. The presentation of the materials are based on my personal study of many national and international reports, books including the World Bank, International Monetary Fund (IMF), Asian Development Bank (ADB), United Nations Development Programme (UNDP) etc.

I hope the book should be useful to the readers in general and academicians in particular and to the people who work in various capacities in the Government and the private sectors.

Finally, I wish to record an appreciation for my wife who inspired me for final printing of the book and helped me in carrying out the proof work of the manuscript.

M Hedayetul Haque

Former Economic Adviser, Ministry of Finance,
Government of Bangladesh
and
Former Economist (Fiscal Policy) of the
Commonwealth Secretariat, London.
Dhaka, July, 2012

About the Author

M Hedayetul Haque graduated with Honours in Economics in 1957 and received a Master's degree in Economics from Dhaka University in 1958. He did postgraduate in Advanced studies in Development Economics courses and theories from the University of Manchester, England with a scholarship provided by the British Government under the Central Treaty

Organization (CENTO) of undivided' Pakistan during September, 1964 October, 1965. He started his career in Narail Victoria College in Jessore (East Pakistan) as lecturer in Economics before he joined the Pakistan central Government service in November, 1959.

Thereafter, he spent decades serving the Government of Pakistan and the Government of Bangladesh in the Ministries of Finance and Economic Affairs/Economic Advisers' wing holding senior position as Assistant Economic Adviser/ Senior Economist, Deputy Economic Adviser, Joint Chief of Bangladesh Civil Service (Economic) and Economic Adviser. While posted as Economic Adviser (1985-92) in the Ministry of Finance, he was appointed by the Commonwealth Secretariat, London as Economist - Fiscal policy as CFTC Expert for a period of 3 years (1992-1995) doing advisory work on fiscal policy issues, projections, analysis and impact on macro-economic performance in the Ministry of Finance, Government of

Tonga in South Pacific in direct liaison with the Commonwealth Secretariat, London.

He received advanced training in the Economic Development Institute of the World Bank, Washington, D.C. USA (1982) on Development Policy Analysis and; Investment Decisions and on Techniques of Economic Analysis courses (1984) of the International Monetary Fund Institute, Washington D.C. USA, Pricing Policy Analysis and issues (1986) in the International Monetary Fund (IMF) Institute, Washington D.C. USA and Government Finance Statistics practices and policy analysis (1991) of the International 'Monetary Fund (IMF) Institute, Washington, D.C., USA held in Canberra (Australia) in conjunction with the Australian Bureau of Statistics. After his retirement from the Government service and successful completion of his assignment with the Commonwealth Secretariat, London he also served as Academic Consultant and Head of the University School of Social Economics and Management (USSEM) - a Training Academy of Social Investment Bank Limited,

Dhaka (1998-2001) and worked on overview of the Development in the Financial sector in Bangladesh in connection with a proposed IDA project as a member of a consultancy team.

During his long service in the Ministry of Finance as Economic Adviser he coordinated the work of macro economic policies and he was responsible for preparation of Annual economic survey work of Bangladesh in the Ministry of Finance for presentation to the Parliament and he was associated with the Budget Reform Committee in the Finance Division as a member. As Economic Adviser he acted as a member of the Panel of Economists for the Third Five year Plan of Bangladesh 1985-86. He worked in close association with the Banks and Financial Institutions. He worked as member/secretary of the Study Group on cost, productivity and profitability etc. of the Nationalized Banks in Bangladesh, 1979. He was a Government Director in a private Bank of Bangladesh (1989-92). He attended /participated in many international meetings, conferences, US AID financed study tour seminars held under the auspices of CENTO and SEATO in undivided Pakistan. He travelled United States of America (USA), United Kingdom (UK) and Australia extensively several times.

Hedayetul was born in village Nawabpur in the district of Mymensingh in a respectable Muslim family of undivided Bengal.

It is with great sadness that the family of the author, M Hedayetul Haque, announced that he passed away in Dhaka, Bangladesh on 10 December 2014, aged 75.

Table of Contents

Development Aspects of Investment - Learning From the Experience of Other Countries

The central activity of the financial institutions in operation at the national and international level is designed to achieve the development goals through macro and micro-investment in all segments of the economy. With their super knowledge, skill, expertise and a store house of experience the financial institutions all over the world have penetrated in the development process through their investment mechanism.

A financial institution has to face a wide range of local conditions besides helping search for solutions for complex processes of development problems and policy initiatives of the Government and various public and private sector agencies. The direction and pace of growth and the way the people share in its benefits depend explicitly on how a country performs the task of management of its investment resources.

Any issue on economic development is primarily concerned with investments in the form of specific projects identification of the most promising projects, in each sector, how to prepare them and carry them forward to successful implementation and then to maintain and operate.

As the cutting edge of development, a project is an important means of marshalling resources, human and material that are available at the national level as these

projects need to be aggregated into a national investment plan wherein a framework of macro-economic
policies are put in place. At the sector level, sector investment strategies and priorities are elaborated along
with supporting policies and at the project level specific projects are identified, prepared and implemented.

A serious concern after World War II for raising the
living standards of at least two-thirds of the people
in the developing world led to international cooperation for development on an unprecedented scale and
dimension that laid the basis for establishing international lending agencies and launching of programs of
bilateral aid to transfer resources and provide technical assistance to many developing countries. In the
process of these activities at the international level,
development economics emerged seeking to identify
the factors stimulating economic growth and designing techniques to overcome that growth.

During all these years after the World War II theories
and doc trines of development economics appeared
quite at rapid pace that resulted in the adoption of

Government policy initiatives related to physical capital formation, balanced economic growth and the "big push", backward linkages, industrialization, rural development, import substitution or export promotion, market based development and investment in human capital with stronger emphasis on basic needs.

Viability of an international financial institution entrusted with the task of carrying out lending activities has always been through adoption of a project approach. As a disciplined way to manage the use of the resources to achieve the development goals, this has assisted the developing countries in achieving orderly economic growth mainly through effecting essential policy changes needed for good project performance and make investments in financially feasible and economically sound projects. It is through project approach that international community has increasingly taken a pragmatic view of development process and development goals. Economic development has proceeded as a long, slow and sometime as painful process of learning from experiences of others.

It is only in the 1950's the development practitioners and academics have increasingly focused on projects as investment package. As an international financial institution, the World Bank has consistently played a practical role in developing and applying the project approach as a disciplined way to analyzing and man aging a set of investment activities. Although in varying proportions projects may include the following elements:

- Capital investment in civil works, equipment or both
- Provision of services for design and engineering, supervision of contraction and improvement of operations and maintenance
- Strengthening of local institutions concerned with implementing and operating the project. including the training of local managers and staff
- Improvements in policies i.e., on pricing, subsidies and cost recovery affecting project performance and the relationship of the both to the sec tor in which it fall and to broader national development objectives

- A plan for implementing the above objectives to achieve the projects objectives within a given time

In the case of institutional financing organization a project is taken as a discrete package of investment policy measures and institutional and other measures designed to achieve a specific development objective within a set period of time.

The boundary line of project and non-project lending is not always easy to draw as the overwhelming proportion of loans and credits of the financial institution, like the World Bank have been for projects. On the international scene, the World Bank has become the largest Lender for development projects. The bank has consistently refined. its approach to project lending. The bank reorganized the need to build up its own qualified staff so it is able to retain its confidence of the banking community. The bank has been a "hands-on" lender being closely involved at all stages i.e., project cycle, assisting borrowers in the Initial selection of projects of completion and the evaluation of the results of the projects. In this way project lending has become a potent instrument for promoting economic growth.

Other multilateral and bilateral lending agencies have followed the Bank's policies and procedures in their own project work or have used Bank appraised projects for their lending. On the whole the project approach that combines sound investment with project related policy and institutional reforms has been a single contribution to the development process throughout the world.

The experience shows that the external lenders including the World Bank tend to select the highest priority projects in the investment program of the borrowing country. What the lending agencies do is that they tend to select the marginal or lowest projects in the investment program of the country concerned. The projects that the Bank helps to finance are invariably changed as a result of the Bank's close involvement in their preparation, appraisal and implementation. The Bank considers that the counsel and advice that it gives to the projects selected are equally important as the transfer of resources. The Bank's project approach is to go to the heart of the development role.

Finally, the financial institutions need to focus not only on individual projects but generally to a review of the national investment program to eliminate projects of low return and provide assistance in setting investment priorities at, the sector level. The Government agencies must, however, be concerned with appropriate analysis of all the projects of the country's investment program not merely with the financing of the donor agencies. With greater flexibility and variety into its lending operations the World Bank's structural adjustment loans were made to countries to assist them in carrying out concrete programs, policy and institutional reform.

A growing number of loans have been concerned primarily with institutional reform of individual sectors or specific policy objectives, such as, fertilizer pricing or liberalization of trade.

The developing countries need to adjust to e recent economic crisis paying greater attention on managing the national economy. Often some countries had cut back on their investment programs. This is all the more important that their scarce resource be used wisely and that their projects work regardless of the form in which international assistance is provided. Commercial bank lending and suppliers' credits to developing countries have often not been linked to sound and productive investments which undoubtedly aggravated the severity of the adjustment process. The need for sound investment planning is more evident in Sub-Saharan Africa which emerged as the region of greatest concern for development because of its persistent poverty, rapidly rising population and declining living standards. The key issue here is that use of investment both domestic and for foreign is in the most effective and appropriate manner.

What the experience has proved is that too much investment restores have gone into projects that have failed to generate significant increases on output. Projects have been selected mostly on political grounds rather than on the basis of net benefits in terms of economic and financial return. Strict adherence to criteria for project selection and design is needed to maximize the return on investment. Therefore, the financing agencies need to take the major responsibility over the use of investment.

For successful development, reasonably efficient and responsive leadership is of paramount importance as there are many services that the Government alone can provide while at the same time recognizing the fact that the public sector has also to meet a growing demand for services within its limited resources availability and capacity to finance.

MANAGEMENT OF NATIONAL INVESTMENT

For management of national investment, the main prerequisites are development planning, establishing the macro-economic policy framework i.e. the pricing policy that conditions the environment in which both public and private investment take place, preparing a public investment program integrating it with the budget, sector analysis covering principal sectors of the economy, agriculture, education, energy, population, health and nutrition, transport, urbanisation, water and sanitation. It seeks to provide background knowledge on the main policy, institutional and investment issues in each sector so essential for the conduct of project implementation work. Then again sector and project analysis interact with each other at least in four principal ways:

Firstly, priorities among individual projects be set based on the objectives, needs and priorities of the sector;

Secondly, how the projects in the sector are designed and carried out through the availability of the institutions, policies and people in the sector having a major impact on the successful implementation of the projects;

Thirdly, various stages of the project cycle from identification of potential projects to evaluation of completed projects;

Fourthly, the dimensions of the project analysis as these apply in various degrees at different stages of the project cycle, technical, economic, financial, social, institutional and environmental analysis;

Finally, procurement and use of consultants needed in the project implementation work. What is made clear is that the appropriate design and execution of investment projects can make an indispensable contribution to economic growth.

Learning from the experience of the international financial institutions like World Bank will have a large impact on economic development the benefits of which an largely be shared equally among all strata of society and hastening the poverty alleviation work.

PROJECT OBJECTIVES AND PROJECT IDENTIFICATION

As already stated a project can be defined as a discrete package of investments, policies and institutional and other actions designed to achieve a specific development objective or a set of objectives within a designated period and a project is likely to comprise several elements. The packaging of investment into distinct projects is an important feature of the lending operations of the financial institutions. Whatever may be the source of finance it is desirable for national planners to organize into project major investments in order to develop a particular region. The discipline of the project approach is very useful when dealing with large number of relatively small investments in a particular region. Then comes the strengthening of the relevant institutions involved with planning and implementing of projects, either financed with the country's own resources or with the external resources. One basic point that needs to be mentioned is the inclusion of policy issues in the project approach as there is a close association between economic policies and project performance. For example, constructing and irrigation project may be the responsibility of the ministry of irrigation or of public works, while achieving the proper level of cost recovery and fixing the appropriate prices for irrigated crops may be the concern of the ministry of finance.

The Project Cycle

There are different stages commonly referred to "project cycle" linked to each other. The commonly used terms of the project cycle are:

Identification

This is the first phase of the cycle i.e., identifying project ideas as these represent a top priority in the use of the country's resources ·targeted to achieve highly important development objective. An initial test of feasibility is needed to ensure that costs are commensurate with the expected benefits and appropriate policies adopted to achieve the goal.

Preparation

After passing through the identification test a firm decision needs to be taken for refinement of the design of the project in all its depth and directions so that the economic, financial, social and institutional aspects of the projects are distinctly well-linked and coordinated through the engineering innovation and design.

APPRAISAL

A formal process of appraisal to assess the formal soundness of the project and its readiness for implementation is needed for gaining approval status of lending agency's loan. In the case of internally generated and financed investment the extent of formal appraisal varies widely from Government to Government. However, before funds are committed, formal appraisal is indeed a prerequisite in the decision making process.

IMPLEMENTATION

The actual development or construction of the project is covered within the implementation stage till the project becomes fully operational. This includes monitoring of all aspects of the work or activity.

EVALUATION

A completed project seeks to determine whether the objectives have been achieved as well as to draw lessons from the experience that can be applied to similar projects in the future. The World Bank has its own machinery to undertake evaluation of projects that it finances while the developing countries have established comprehensive system for evaluating the results of their project evaluation. The project approach has proved a potent instrument for rationalizing and improving the investment process. Its principal advantage lies in providing a logical framework, investment priorities established, project alternatives considered and sector policy issues addressed. It imposes a discipline on planners and decision makers. Further, it ensures that relevant problems and issues are taken into account and subjected to systematic analysis before decisions are reached and implemented. If this can be correctly applied, this will greatly enhance the development impact of country's scarce resources.

However, the limitations of the project approach are there as the project approach depends on estimates and forecasts which may be subject to human error. Through the project approach, value judgments can be made explicitly. Although there are risks involved in project approach which can be assessed but not avoided, the basic work is that the projects need to be designed and implemented against the political, social and economic changes that may occur.

Finally, the effectiveness of the project approach depends on the skill and judgments of the users. In spite of the pitfalls the policy makers and decision makers need to use this to take advantage of this approach tactfully and judiciously.

CHAPTER 2

Development Economics and Evaluation of Activities under International System

Development of human resources is a development paradigm. Inherent idea within the broad concept of development is creation of an environment in which people in general have ample opportunities to develop their full potentiality to lead productive and creative lives to suit the needs of diverse interests and aspirations. In this comprehensive aspect of development lies a bigger horizon of choices that people can find their ways to deploy their ingenuity for freer activity to increase their creativity and wealth.

Building of human capabilities is fundamental to enlarging these choices. These choices are to lead long, healthy and fruitful lives and to have access to the resources needed for a decent standard of living and fully and effectively participate in the life of the community. Without these human capabilities many opportunities in life remain outside the domain of human life and enjoyment. Real development is often forgotten as people concern themselves with merely accumulation of financial assets and commodities rather than human welfare as the end of development. The goal of human development is human freedom so essential and vital for pursuing capabilities and realizing rights. If people are free to exercise choices and participate in decision making process, then human development and human rights help secure the well-being and dignity of all people building self-respect and the respect of others.

HUMAN CAPACITY ADVANCEMENT AND MDGs

Strengthening human capacity for bringing about positive change in improving lives is the goal of development efforts undertaken by many national and international development institutions including the United Nations, UNDP, World Bank, ADB etc.

This is also a great promise for developing countries in their efforts to achieve the Millennium Development Goals (MDGs) through:

- Eradicate extreme poverty and hunger
- Addressing universal primary education
- Promote gender equality and empower women
- Reduce child mortality
- Improve maternal health
- Combating HIV/AIDS, malaria and other diseases
- Ensuring environmental sustainability
- Develop a global partnership of development

In early 2007 the world economy experienced exceptionally rapid growth having a positive impact on poverty reduction in general and on the performance of the least developed countries, in particular Sub-Saharan African countries growing at an average of more than six per cent in 2007.

A large number of emerging countries of the south east region led by China have demonstrated capacity for economic advancement in the quickest possible time towards reducing poverty and achieving MDGs. Global economy is recently facing a serious financial crisis and unprecedented uncertainty attributed to persistent strains in US financial markets further hitting the economy in the midst of rising prices for energy and food.

With the elevated inflation risks in the US and advanced economies now threatening the global economy the developing countries are likely to face a major setback for poverty reduction. This situation to help solve the revival of the financial sector compounded by expansionary macro-economic policies in many countries further exacerbated the inflationary up-surge throughout the world economy.

The trend of the global economy highlights the fact that the countries are interdependent and needs to initiate global policies consistent with their own particular set of challenges. International donor assistance directed towards improving the capacity of the people and the institutions is at the centre of development challenge: poverty reduction, achievement of MDGs, democratic governance, crisis prevention and recovery, environment and sustainable development.

CAPACITY DEVELOPMENT AND IMPROVING LIVES

Capacity development is the process through which people in general, organizations and societies in order to achieve real gains obtain, strengthen and maintain the capabilities to set and achieve the development objectives. The United Nations and many other organizations work alongside Governments, civil society and other organizations are striving to promote human development by helping people to access the knowledge, experience and resources that they need to lead a better and comfortable standard of living. Considering capacity development as the main target of development process - UNDPs main source of guidance for engaging with development partners, the Strategic Plan: 2008-2011 stipulates that all of UNDPs policy advice, technical support, advocacy and contributions to strengthening coherence in global development must aim for real improvements in people's lives and in the choices and opportunities open to them.

In the perspective of experience what is observed is that improvements in lives, choices and opportunities are easier to come by for some countries than others. Some developing countries are benefiting from globalization and catching up with the richest countries, while hundreds of millions of people remain excluded from the benefits of growth. Some countries and regions are falling behind and even within countries with strong economic performance, significant pockets of exclusion can be found.

The world economy faces a financial sector induced slow down the length of which is uncertain. The role of the United Nations organizations remains to help accelerate progress in those countries that are catching up quickly to the rich world while helping to catalyze progress in those parts of the world that are lagging behind. The way in which this does is by helping to build effective institutions that can deliver the benefits of growth and development to all people particularly the poorest.

The world today is just half way to the 2015 the target date for achieving the MDGs. Compared to the year 2000 the number of children that die each year of preventable causes has fallen by some three million enrolment in primary schools is up worldwide, an additional two million people receive treatment for AIDS, and women now occupy a significantly higher percentage of seat in parliaments.

Today in spite of many shortfalls many countries are demonstrating that rapid and large scale progress is possible in spite of many constraints. But it can take place where strong Government leadership, good policies that support private investment and productivity growth and sound strategies for scaling up public investments are reinforced by adequate financial and technical support from the international community.

In these general revolutionary efforts for upliftment of human destiny many countries of Asia have led the way with the fastest reduction in extreme poverty in human history. Though the progress is visible many countries still remain off track, particularly across large parts of Africa and among the least developed countries. Some of the fast growing countries of south Asia face serious challenges in improving nutrition and achieving certain other goals.

Some of the middle income countries in Latin America have struggled to wipe out pockets of extreme poverty which has declined overall but adjustments in purchasing power estimates are expected to lead to downward revisions in the levels of real income in many countries. Achieving the MDGs goals requires that the existing commitments by developing and developed countries are followed through. At the same time progress that has been achieved toward the MDGs could be compromised in the absence of a comprehensive coordinated response to climate change.

One of the generations major development challenges - global warming could bring about serious reversals in poverty reduction, nutrition, health and education. The most immediate and devastating impact would be felt by the world's poorest i.e. those least responsible for the greenhouse emissions and high rates of carbon emitting energy consumption which basically are at the root of the problem. These problems are paramount while facing the development challenges.

What is necessary is to scale up the work of the United Nations agency in organizational capacity support strengthening institutions to empower the citizens they serve. It should work to support institutions that safeguard political and economic stability and security, promote the equitable distribution of resources, and increase public transparency and accountability and enhance the conditions for sustainable human development. But this support needs to come not as support in isolation but as a trusted partner in development work. Any such organization should forge partnerships across diverse spheres of influence, from national, municipal and local Government bodies to non-Government and civil society organizations including grassroots coalitions, faith based groups, academia as well as private sector and international donors. In all these areas priority needs are on maximizing local resources and fostering collaboration among various partners of development work. This includes strong engagement with CSOs (civil society organizations) as these are critical to national ownership, accountability, good governance, decentralization, democratization of development cooperatives or societies and the quality and relevance of official development programs.

SUSTAINABLE BUSINESS INVESTMENT

Growing sustainable business through a platform of companies to engage in pro-poor countries with a challenging business environment may be given a priority in the global context. While looking beyond social investments and philanthropy, such a platform offers national and international companies a distinct path to develop commercially viable business projects with a view to increasing profitability and or engaging in new markets. Such a program will ensure encouraging trends in capacity development efforts in the countries development efforts and in the management of programs related to finance, procurement and human resources.

Another encouraging result will be an evolution of civil service reform, building of specialized skills and qualified leadership, development of incentive systems and introducing mechanisms for reinforcing ethical standards as well as anti-corruption measures. Still there should be renewed emphasis on continued learning and on tertiary education. This coupled with innovative responses to brain drain in critical sectors aiming to tap into the benefits of an increasingly mobile global labor market will facilitate increasing benefits instead of growing hazards and uncertainty in this sector.

Advancing towards the development goals the partnership of the countries with the international system enables them to play larger responsibility with the global development program. The new members of the European Union should also be encouraged to play a greater role in providing development assistance.

In all these work under the international system, flexibility and adaptability must be given a priority consideration as essential components in the capacity improvement. Any development program under the international system including those of the United Nations needs to be directed to work with the middle income countries who are often challenged to make optimal use of their human and financial capital distributing their resources efficiently through sound planning. Such work to engage the middle income countries by supporting capacity development at subnational levels, such as, working with municipal and district administration bodies in regard to the improvement of integrated planning, managing development finance and boosting implementation capacities for local service delivery must continue with utmost speed and capability to capture a larger segment of the population.

Side by side the international organizations should extend their support to the policy makers of the developing countries in strengthening responses to a variety of areas, such as, climate change, promoting gender equality as well as supporting and strengthening marginalized populations and state institutions. Any international approach to capacity development must meet the challenges beyond the individual project delivery to address the institutional capacity to contribute to the global push to transform people's lives to a better and still higher standard of living through newly generated sources of income. What the international organization like the United Nations must do is to create a family environment to mobilize political will and hold the leaders to their commitment for making available the resources needed for the millennium development goals.

CHAPTER 3

Economic Contents in the Analysis of Development Projects

W hat are the economic aspects in the analysis of projects in true perspective and how to proceed with the goal of achieving maximum gains with minimum risk, minimum costs and limited available resources is the theme of this paper. The basic economic choice in all developing countries that has appeared prominently is concerned with the decisions affecting the size and composition of investments in individual sectors with particular reference to economic rates of return through cost-benefit analysis a critical element in decision making process of investments.

One of the means to help guide the policy makers in making judicious investments decisions in a systematic and consistent manner is the cost-benefit technique. This technique helps us to understand whether on balance investment program that is undertaken is worthwhile or not in respect of location, timing, scale, composition, technology or method of implementation, objectives set forth including other factors i.e. whether the policy environment is conducive to its implementation and operation.

In fact, through the cost-benefit analysis we know whether the project can yield a reasonable rate of return to the economy or there is still other alternative means of achieving still higher rate of return. This technique has been largely applied by international aid agencies and in most projects financed by the World Bank, regional banks and many other bilateral and multilateral institutions. Many developing countries are subjected to this kind of analysis for which they have separate established units in their economic and social management system.

While looking into the conceptual aspects of the measurement of the cost and benefits of a project, the pertinent questions that arise are: who are the decision makers and what the objectives are. For example, a particular decision viewed from individuals will differ materially from a decision taken from the societal point of view. To the extent a particular project, say, establishment of a technical institute may be profitable to the students but from the standpoint of society this may not be profitable as a whole in terms of the costs incurred by society. Hence the essential difference between financial and economic analysis of projects.

The basic problem is setting objectives of a project to determine how the projects costs and benefits are defined so that anything affecting the objectives adversely is a cost and anything that promotes them is a benefit. But, in reality, this may not be the case. A policy maker or a decision maker is to make out a case out of a multiplicity of conflicting and interrelated objectives. Just like a business firm which wishes to maximize net profits and minimize risks a country has to set its target to increase national income, to reduce income inequalities, reduce unemployment and through self-reliance strengthen national security. There may be a host of many other objectives which the cost-benefit analysis can accommodate though having difficulties in making good trade-offs among the various objectives. It becomes, therefore, essentially incumbent on the authority to focus attention on the principal objectives - maximization of national income for the country as a whole while in the case of individuals or business enterprises, cost benefit analysis takes profit maximization as a sole objective.

A recent innovation is so called social benefit analysis to include considerations of income distribution and the national savings rate. Given the political context, the cost-benefit analysis may help the decision makers to crystallize their values and objectives. In reality, the relevance and utility of this analysis mostly depend on the consistency between the decision maker's objectives and the trade-offs among them as these are truly reflected in it. Hence the need for considerations of alternative techniques as an essential feature of project preparation and design.

In many World Bank and multilateral aid agencies projects there is a great deal of apathy in the identification and proper weighing of alternatives due to which the out turn of the projects is negative and the projects do not yield substantially higher return in terms of income growth and employment. Technical options should be compared and the best alternative selected. For example, to use steam, diesel or diesel electric locomotive or to expand a railway line or to build a parallel road should be compared with each other and the best alternative selected. If, for example, different technologies can produce the same output or benefit both in quantity and quality, then the analysis should identify the least cost alternatives through comparison of the investment and operating costs. If, for example, both benefits and costs vary among alternatives, then each alternative with its cost and benefit streams must be assessed separately so that the highest net benefit can be selected.

COMPARABLE SITUATION WITH OR WITHOUT THE PROJECT

Without the project, availability of inputs and outputs in one sector and their utilization in another sector or in the rest of the economy would have been different. A comparable situation i.e. with or without project is a basic measurement of the additional benefits attributable to a project. For examples, in agricultural projects, cropping patterns, yields, output levels and commodity prices change substantially from the base levels even without the project due to market conditions or other factors while in projects, such as, modernization of a plant or expansion of highway may have as their primary objective to prevent future in-creases in costs or decreases in benefits in the form of deterioration of existing capacity, increasing conges-tion or declining quality of service.

Thus, in the case of without project, the factors, like, expected cost increases or benefit decreases need to be taken into consideration so as to reflect the changes brought about by the project. For an accu-rate comparison of the situations i.e. with and without the project this calls for difficult judgements. For ex-ample, projects intended to increase capacity in the case of industrial plants, power generation, sea ports, and railways etc. not undertaking projects means do-ing without such increments to capacity. If, on the other hand, when the projects purpose is to reduce unit costs or to improve the quality of service i.e. ag-ricultural extension or health care not undertaking projects means foregoing these benefits. However, the problems may arise due to appropriate assumptions to be made about the operating practices and policies of the Government.

DEMAND ANALYSIS AND FORECASTING

For cost-benefit analysis, the analysis of demand for the output of a project helps to determine the revenues or benefits to be obtained from undertaking of the project and in what scale. This applies for example, to most industrial and agricultural production projects, whether or not output is sold. Although demand analysis is basic to the assessment of a project potentiality, this is not done in the effective way so that the project planners must not assume that a market for the output of a project exists.

Necessary investigation as to the composition of demand and price elasticity sector wise should be carried out. Demand forecasts often turn out to be faulty and defective. Often long range forecasting gives a negative result as predicting changes in technology, income behavior and other factors change previous pattern and affecting basic assumptions of a forecast becomes uncertain and mostly difficult. Besides, data required for forecasting is often a questionable quality limiting the forecasters' choice of technique; while ad hoc collection of data is expensive that necessitates to be done in the most cost effective manner.

In most projects, it must be understood that the decision to be made have long-term consequences. For example, in transport or in major industrial or power projects, investments may be large, lumpy and irreversible. In terms of other investment opportunities, there may be errors in respect of size, timing or location of projects. Therefore, demand forecasts being an essential part of the decision making process, it should be rational. The preparation of a demand forecast must be done taking into account the cost of using various techniques i.e. the cost of preparing the forecast and the cost resulting from an incorrect forecast. The trade-off between these will vary from sector to sector along with the size of project investment.

A large commitment of resources may lead to greater accuracy up to a certain limit but beyond that increased accuracy may lead to increased cost. However, the forecaster after producing his best estimate of likely demand should carry out a sensitivity test of the cost benefit analysis.

The advantage of this test is that it assists the project planners in providing with safeguards against some eventualities. Demand forecasts also need to be updated on a regular basis during the preparation and initial operation of the project so that a consistency is maintained between forecasts and real situation. Both benefits as well as costs of projects are spread over a long period so that these two variables differ greatly from one project to another. The concept of time preference is that values received earlier are worth more than values received later. In order to make the values realized at different points of time comparable the technique developed is known as the time discounting technique. The effect of time consuming depends on how costs and benefits are distributed over time and also on the discount rate which can help the decision makers to apply their time preference in choosing among projects. The problem is to choose the appropriate discount rate also referred to as the opportunity cost of capital i.e. returns available in domestic and international capital markets. The alternative approach is to use the national income data over a period of years to estimate average returns on investment. While in many countries estimates of incremental capital output ratios are available as a tool for macro-economic planning, another approach is to consider rates of return on a sample of projects of the past or those estimated over the next few years.

None of the above approaches, however, do not provide a satisfactory solution. Market interest rates may not be good indicator of the cost of capital due to distortions, such as, regulated interest rates, fragmented capital markets, credit rationing etc. prevalent in most of the developing countries.

On the other hand, estimates from the national income data may be unreliable due to difficulties in apportioning increases in national income to different contributing factors. The notional concept is, therefore, the discount rate or the opportunity cost of capital. It may be possible to have pretty good idea of the range of yields on alternative investments and therefore, of the discount rate in a particular country. May be that certain discount rates, for example, 5 per cent while others at 20 per cent would be too high? In the analysis of projects the opportunity cost of capital is usually taken to be of the order of 10 per cent a year (net of inflation) varying among countries at different stages of development.

The opportunity cost of a resource deployed in a particular way is to an individual or enterprise are usually the financial expenditure defined as the value it could command if it were used in the best available alternative; it thus playing as a powerful concept and a central role in cost-benefit analysis. This concept is applied in all economic systems having market oriented, centrally planned or a mixture of the two and to all objectives of profit maximization or promotion of national welfare. Measuring the cost and benefits of a project to an individual or enterprise are usually the financial expenditure for acquiring the goods and services needed to establish and operate the project, while the benefits are the funds received for the goods and services produced by the project. The expected market prices for these goods and services are also taken as the appropriate opportunity cost for estimating the costs and benefits to the enterprise. The market prices for inputs and outputs may, however, not be an acceptable measure of the true costs and benefits while measuring the profitability of project from the societal point of view. As the market prices of inputs and outputs are often distorted by various taxes, subsidies, quotas, regulatory measures, the shadow prices are employed to deal with this problem. While using a good or service as a project input will mean either diverting that input from other uses or increasing the production or import or both.

Applying for a specific situation the shadow price of the input will be either its value in the alternative use (the opportunity cost) or the cost of augmenting the supply (the marginal cost of production or import) or weighted average of the two. In the same way, the output of a project, besides helping increase of consumption or export is likely to lead to closing down less efficient production facilities. Now the shadow price of the output will be measured by the benefits received from the increased supply and the cost that can be avoided or a combination of the two. There are practical difficulties in application of these principles to arrive at an appropriate estimation that would also include consideration of the need to understand the production possibilities and valuing the various goods and services in different applications. In order to keep the problem manageable the project inputs and outputs may be land.

CHAPTER 4

Financial Aspects of Project Analysis and Implementation in Developing Countries

All developing countries have almost a common approach and constraints in financial apprais-al, analysis and implementation of all types of devel-opment projects whether these are revenue earning ventures or not. Drawing up a financing plan, as a first step, applies to all types of projects and this is an integral part of project preparation in order to ensure that sufficient funds are available either from within or abroad with which to operate and complete the project. The financing needs of the project are generally broken down into two components: foreign exchange and local currency expenditures. While the external funding is intended to cover foreign exchange costs identified in the project's cost estimate, the terms and conditions of such financing are divergent to the extent of its source- aid organizations, commercial banks or suppliers' credits, these need distinct identification. The donor agencies often place limits on the proportion of a project's cost varying from country to country depending upon the type of project willing to finance. In case of co-financing by external aid agencies, a residual of local currency costs and often foreign costs need to be financed by internally generated sources. Often the external agencies are reluctant to finance cost overruns either in local currency or in foreign currency in which case the borrowing entity has to take the responsibility of financing such overruns.

A reliable estimate of project costs is, thus, all the more important based on detailed design and engineering work to be undertaken with due allowances for physical and price variations that may occur in the course of the project operation. To ensure availability of adequate funds in the operating phase of the project it is essential that this aspect is accorded priority. Recurrent cost obligations are often underestimated and totally ignored with the result that facilities once completed deteriorate due to non-availability of funds for operating and maintenance of the project.

Different projects have different level of operational and maintenance costs. For example, construction of new schools as well as health sector need to incur substantial recurrent costs for salaries and for maintaining and operating the facilities whereas the construction of irrigation canals and highways need substantial routine and periodic investigations and maintenance for which appropriate funds and organizational arrangements need to be provided along with the decisions as to depreciation and replacement of machinery. All projects except those involving revenue enterprises are dependent on domestic budgetary resources for which decision makers have to have a clear view of the long term budgetary implications. Thus, a project's fiscal impact should take into account any flow of resources attributed to the project through user charges.

Budgetary resources are sometimes earmarked to finance particular investments or may be requested by external lenders. Besides, revolving funds at the outset of the project and replenished at periodic intervals are a useful method for making funds readily available that help a quick start in implementing a project of so much importance for the economy. However, as a whole, this is not a substitute for sound budgetary practices in regard to the public investment program. However, whatever the project, a minimum of financial information and reporting will be necessary to keep track of the progress as to how the expenditures have been incurred or whether the project is on schedule and the cost estimates are done accurately and strictly adhered to.

The Government ministries often fail to maintain minimum standard in the accounts necessitating an independent review, audit and examination by a separate public agency. Besides the need for adequacy of funds for carrying out successful implementation of projects the financial situation of the users or beneficiaries are also pertinent issues for consideration before launching a project. Projects like water supply or any urban development project will need to assess the ability of the consumers to afford the charges to be imposed on them. In case of agricultural development project, for example, it is necessary to have a cash flow analysis drawing up a model farm budget to ensure that the cash inflow of such a project exceeds the cash outflow inclusive of debt repayment, if any, in the initial period of changes and innovation of the project in question and providing for risks of additional labor and capital as well as unforeseen management costs.

COST RECOVERY POLICY OF PROJECTS

Cost recovery policy is a vital aspect of project preparation from the point of view of the accepted principle of equity. These costs need to be recovered from the users in the form of price changes, taxes or specific charges in order that the projects do not create in return a privileged class of beneficiaries through income transfer or some form of subsidy while depriving the rest of the community of the product or service. As part of the financial analysis of projects three essential ingredients need to be distinctly identified: These are:

- economic efficiency,
- income distribution and
- revenue generation.

Economic efficiency is basically concerned with the pricing policy for efficient use of resources to maximize net benefit to the economy, any deviation from the efficiency pricing will result in underutilization of industrial or infrastructure capacity. In urban or rural projects, for instance, economic benefits to the society will be minimal as a result of inappropriate farm technologies or congested urban highways. Since an efficient pricing is governed by the marginal cost rule modifications are essential to allow for various complications on account of substantial costs incurred in charging for various services, for example, taking meter reading or collection of road tolls or in adjusting prices to reflect costs, current prices to reflect future demand of the consumers, problems arising from capital investment, expected price changes of close substitutes, reflection of external diseconomies in prices. Thus, an effective pricing to recover costs is wholly dependent on other factors varying from sector to sector beyond the control of the authority.

Another national objective is to improve income distribution in which case cost recovery policy through efficiency pricing is not appropriate. Differences in income level have to be taken into account before the changes in prices are introduced and other charges levied strictly in accordance with the ability of the beneficiaries of the project in question. While it may be desirable to charge small farmers less than the large farmers for each unit of services extended under the same project, for others like the water supply projects some allowance can be made through a surcharge on larger consumers intended to benefit the small users having the need for minimum water consumption close to the lifeline requirement.

Although equity is served by making user charges or taxes progressive but, in practice, considerations, such as, any negative effect on people's incentive to participate in the project, tax evasion and the cost of collection may limit the prospect of this approach. The pricing and taxation policies also need to take into consideration the distinction between equity through equal distribution of income and equity in the sense of fairness. The later refers to the uniform pricing for all consumers and that taxes should be proportional to the benefits received. In this sense, fairness tends to conflict with the criteria of both efficiency and income distribution not making allowances for disparities in the cost of supplying different consumers at different levels of income level.

A cost recovery policy has also to take into consideration that many Governments are short of fiscal resources at their disposal. The collection of revenue is often less than the minimum required for operating costs and to recover full investment of the project. This may not be the case in which the Government is in a stronger financial position but when the fiscal resources are at a premium the Government finds no alternative but to collect more revenue rather than depending only on the efficiency pricing mechanism. A cost recovery policy in a rural or urban development project will help the Government to mobilize the resources with which to replicate the project and extend its benefits to more of the needy. A well-designed project will often increase the income or welfare of the beneficiaries so that a substantial level of cost recovery can be justified either on equity or on fiscal grounds.

An ideal cost recovery is one that that secures maximum economic benefits from the project taking into account its impact on the distribution of benefits and on Government and enterprise finances. The goal of the project should be to recover part of the costs or even full costs plus some additional part of the benefits recognizing the fact that there are difficult trade-offs to be made among the efficiency, equity and revenue objectives, more so in the poorer countries who have to make more painful and difficult choices.

OVERVIEW OF FINANCIAL ASPECTS

Above is an overview of a few financial aspects of project preparation that necessitates designing a cost recovery instruments. Since the impact of a project on public savings and or any increase in public revenue consequent upon implementation of a project will have an important bearing on the cost recovery the instruments designed should be selective specifically targeted to the beneficiary group. There are two instruments that meet this test:

- The first is the price charged for the product or service supplied by the project entity. Pricing can be used not only to promote economic efficiency but also to extract larger or smaller payments from the users or beneficiaries.

- The second instrument is so called benefit tax, that is, for example, on improved land that bears largely on project beneficiaries.

However, designing a benefit tax although quite a demanding task, it should be possible to identify the beneficiaries and classify them into income groups. Any additional income received by a beneficiary from the project needs to be estimated as well net of all incremental payments on existing taxes. Further, for reflection of equity considerations, judgements in respect of the weights for valuing consumption gains of each income group need to be made for different income groups. Besides, the adverse effects of benefit taxes on the production incentives need to be considered so that these are kept at a minimum level. With these complexities the designing benefit taxes may be a difficult proposition discriminating among people of different income levels that leads one to the conclusion that a uniform benefit tax is the alternative best choice.

These practical limitations to cost recovery either through prices or benefit taxes help us to understand that the objectives of efficiency, equity and income generation vary widely among different sectors of the economy depending on the nature of the projects under implementation. The sectors, like education or public health recovery from the beneficiaries not playing a significant role, this approach is intended in the interest of mobilizing additional funds. In many other sectors, such as, power, telecommunications, ports, railways, manufacturing industries etc. efficiency pricing is the starting point while considerations of income distribution can usually be implemented through different charges. In sectors, like, power, telecommunications, ports and industry economics of large scale production favorable market conditions make it often possible to achieve full cost recovery.

In the interest of low income target groups the projects that are undertaken, such as, for example, upgrading of slums, sites and services, rural development, water supply and sanitation projects, there remains a little scope for establishing system that would ensure efficiency pricing. For such projects charges imposed on beneficiaries will depend primarily on income distribution considerations within limits. A minimal user charge will help generate some revenue just to prevent overuse of a free good or service.

Although a high level of cost recovery has often been achieved in many development projects in the urban sector in developing countries financed by the national and international organizations, the countries at low income level need to adopt cautious and pragmatic steps for successful preparation and implementation of projects suited to their own needs and environment.

CHAPTER 5

Fiscal Policy Implications in Developing Countries and Stabilization Program in the Context of Structural Adjustment

FISCAL AND MACRO-ECONOMIC POLICIES

Fiscal policies have been a focus of interest in all macro-economic policy decisions of the Government.

In recent years its importance has increased and its coverage has been extended over a wider horizon with the growth of various financial instruments, intermediaries and financial environment in which economic policies are implemented and put into operation to achieve both short-term and long term goals. The fiscal policy is just one aspect of economic policy, although a major policy variable deter mining macro-economic performance necessitating an efficient and effective working of other policy instruments including monetary, financial etc. The fiscal policy and fiscal deficits or surplus are closely integrated whose combined effects, in the first instance, fall on either aggregate demand or aggregate supply with the consequent impact on the movement of domestic prices and on the level of economic activity and later on, transmitted to the position of external balance which have been at the core of stabilisation program of Government of the developing countries. In recent years many studies have been made in regard to the role of fiscal policies in promoting. Growth and in sustaining the development process through improvement in the quantity of investment and savings. There has been a growing concern, particularly in view of macro and micro disequilibria in the economy that stabilization programs alone would not induce satisfactory growth and development.

EXTERNAL SHOCKS AND THE FISCAL SECTOR

In the developing world critical problems arise particularly from the growing external shocks which are often so frequent and of such magnitude having direct implications and consequences for the fiscal sector. These consequences are so great particularly in countries mostly dependent on taxation of international trade having undeveloped tax systems. These external shocks are so severe and unpredictable that it becomes often critical in formulating and often in executing fiscal policy especially in such developing countries. As such, there is an increasing interest in devising analytical tools to formulate proper responses to developments in the external sector.

As fiscal policies are essentially and critically integrated with other economic policy instruments, any lack of credibility of fiscal policy in the developing countries can cause capital flight with consequent deterioration in the external balance. External policy instruments, such as, exchange rates, tariffs and subsidies and trade liberalization have substantial and perceptible implications for the fiscal policies pursued by any Government. In view of the wider implications the international organizations, such as IMF and the World Bank have, in particular, given serious thought in providing analysis in the financial planning process and implementation in their adjustment programs for the developing countries.

STABILITY AND GROWTH

A critical role of the fiscal policy issues is in attaining and sustaining stability and growth although the latter are sometimes conflicting and complementary as stability is a precondition for sustained growth. In the efforts to attain and sustain macro-economic stability the Government often tries to reduce excess aggregate demand in the economy which can be facilitated by means of a sustained growth in income and employment. In spite of these stated correlation between stability and growth the policies initiated in the developing countries to promote growth often stand in the way of attaining stability. While the fiscal policies ate adapted to increase or decrease aggregate demand, they also often become a source of economic imbalance and instability. What is necessary is to enhance the complementary relationship between stabilization and growth and, in fact, this is a critical issue in the policy making decisions.

While a number of fiscal policy instruments can reduce a budget deficit in the short run, each instrument needs to be assessed on the basis of its ability to increase potential output hat can bring about a durable fiscal adjustment. This strengthening can make the stabilization program more durable by facilitating the current fiscal adjustment and by reducing the required future fiscal adjustment. Thus, by properly combining stabilization with structural policies an economy could grow out of its Government debt. A relaxation of fiscal adjustment is an essential condition to improve the quality of its stabilization program.

LOW LEVEL OF SAVINGS AND INVESTMENT

A critical bottleneck in the growth process in developing countries is the low level of domestic savings which is due to the insufficient rates of return to capital and the absence of both well-functioning capital markets and institutions to compensate for the risks involved in saving and investment activities tending to dampen the propensity to save and invest. The tax system being traditional although designed to induce increases in domestic savings are also ineffective as the interest elasticity of saving is low. In this context there is a need to address possible fiscal policy roles in promoting savings in such an environment. There are theoretical and empirical studies which show the limitations of tax policy suggesting alternative uses of fiscal policy which needs to be designed to create a planned budgetary surplus so that the surplus so generated can be channelled into productive investment activities.

FISCAL RIGIDITIES, PUBLIC DEBT AND CAPITAL FLIGHT

In the analysis of fiscal rigidities, public debt and capital flight in many developing countries it has been observed that often fiscal rigidities and lack of an appropriate standard and discipline in the working of the fiscal system and policies present a critical situation which have caused capital flight without any limit to the detriment of smooth and efficient functioning of the economy. In such an unstable setting of the economy the Government is said to have a weak fiscal discipline which result in a large fiscal imbalances. In such a situation a general expectation of the people is that the fiscal imbalance is inevitably financed through inflationary expectations. These expectations have often induced the domestic bond holders to purchase foreign bonds to finance the external imbalance. These have caused capital flight until such time credible fiscal discipline is ensured. In the context of fiscal policies the Government needs to put greater attention to control high inflation as the latter has not only critical allocative and distributional implications but is also detrimental to the growth process. The policy of disinflation and stabilization will not by themselves be able to provide long-term benefits without the use of fiscal policies to control or eliminate the sources of high growth of inflation. Without the Government's cautious efforts in this direction various element i.e. freezes, controls and income policies that often work in an economy will not only result in economic costs but also political and administrative costs to the detriment of the long term growth of the economy.

Impact of Unpredictable Shocks on the Fiscal Sector

Many developing countries since the early 1970s' experienced unpredictable shock as the aggregate economic activity and domestic prices in industrial countries become much more volatile compared to the earlier period. Also the world price of oil and non-oil commodities, the value of major currencies and the world interest rates become highly unstable. Further, after the abandonment of fixed exchange rates the fluctuations in the value of key currencies made the effective exchange rates of developing countries much more unstable depending on the major currencies to which their currencies are pegged. These fluctuations in the exchange rates having direct adverse consequences in the current account put serious strain in the fiscal sector of many developing countries. These external shocks intensified the fluctuations in Government revenue and foreign grants and often the availability and the conditions for financing. Also the external shocks have elicited diverse fiscal policy reactions having different degrees of success in neutralizing the impact of the shocks on the domestic economy. There has been a considerable research and investigations in recent years as the factors associated with external shocks and their impact on fiscal variables and various measures taken by the Government in the fiscal side which generally are of three kinds:

- a decrease in debt,
- an increase in public investment, and
- an increase in public expenditure.

There are also alternative policy responses to declining revenue which are a reduction in public investment and an increase in public expenditure. There are also alternative policy responses to declining revenue which are a reduction in public spending and an increase in domestic borrowing. While there are limitations of various fiscal policy instruments in developing countries consequences of the cuts in public spending at a time of negative external shock can be mitigated only through improved efficiency.

Recent experiences of many developing countries have shown that aggregate Government expenditure have responded to both the anticipated and unanticipated components of external shocks. An unexpected downturn in revenue earning without timely actions to formulate and execute effective fiscal policy responses pose serious problems for the developing countries. In this situation the Government should take a long-term view in formulating and executing fiscal stabilization programs.

FISCAL POLICY LINKAGES

The role of fiscal policy and its linkages with the monetary and external policies are critical in the decision making process of economic policies. This is more so as the bank financing of Government deficits is a significant source of inflation in many countries. This method of financing besides providing a direct linkage between fiscal and monetary policies affect the external balance through their impact on aggregate demand, on the domestic saving and investment balance and on individual taxes and subsidies. In analyzing the conventional methods of finance there are three critical parameters:

- the price elasticity of the tax system;
- the ratio of tax revenue to national income; and
- the ratio of the money supply to national income

PARAMETERS IN THE EXPENDITURE SIDE

In the spending side of the Government the important parameters are the real interest rates and the liquidity constraint consumer behavior. The dominance of the liquidity constraints relative to the interest rates is the key element in the determination of savings and this is more pronounced in the low income countries than in other developing countries. This situation where domestic saving is largely responsive to the real positive rate of interest suggests that in order to increase the level of domestic saving in the low income countries it is necessary to bring about large changes in the rate of interest.

FISCAL DIMENSION OF TRADE POLICY

One final aspect of the fiscal policy is the conflict between and complementarity of fiscal and external policy instruments. In other words, the fiscal dimensions of foreign trade policy focus on two important aspects of the policy interaction: the first one relates to the efficiency with which taxes in the foreign trade sector are enforced in the presence of the factors, such as, the cost of tax collection and the policy objectives of the tax like revenue, protection and market failure. Even considering these aspects the general conclusion is that the share of foreign trade taxes in the optimal tax basket is still much lower than the share of foreign trade taxes in many developing countries. The second aspect of the fiscal policy in foreign trade taxation is its static and dynamic role in the external adjustment process focussing on the impact of fiscal policy instruments on the external balance under fixed and fixable exchange regimes.

The budgetary impact on the external balance of the economy is estimated on the basis of the import demand generated through both the impact of expenditure on domestic absorption and the impact of blank financing of the deficit through its impact on the money supply and domestic prices. As the budget is affected by imports through their impact on tariffs, the budgetary impact on the external balance of a country is dependent on the size of revenue derived from the import tariffs.

Fiscal policy plays decisive role in promoting and sustaining stabilization and growth in developing countries. The crucial roles of the fiscal policy emphasize the importance of considering and in-depth analysis of the dose inter-dependence between fiscal, monetary and external sector polices.

In the background of the experiences of the 1970s and 1980s, our conclusion is that stabilization and adjustment are necessary conditions for growth indicating further that efficient structural measures are not only essential conditions but also these are of crucial importance in mobilizing domestic and foreign savings for attainment of sustained rate of growth.

The overall experience in the last decades have provided further evidence about the implications of the volatile external environment for the fiscal sector in developing countries as well as the impact of fiscal policy on the external sector.

BUDGETARY IMPLICATION OF STRUCTURAL MEASURES

The fiscal policy issues are many that deserve the attention of the researchers and the fiscal analysts. The issues that need to be investigated and analysed relate to the budgetary implication of structural measures both in the fiscal and non-fiscal areas, such as, the short and long run impacts on the fiscal balance of structural reforms in goods, labor, money, capital markets and trade liberalization. Effects of uncertainty on the performance of the fiscal sector and on fiscal discipline are equally useful to study how the level of Government expenditure is planned in the face of uncertainty as to the magnitude of Government revenue and the way these plans or estimates are revised.

Of particular interest to study is how a political consensus on various fiscal policy measures, in general and on the fiscal policy stance, in particular, are reached as well as the roles of both public and financial institutions; and in the design and implementation of specific fiscal policy adjustment, the methodology adopted to measure and assess the impact of fiscal stance in a country's particular situation is of paramount importance.

FISCAL POLICY AND STABILIZATION

Stabilization programs include a viable balance of payments at least over the medium term, promotion of economic growth in a stable economic environment, stability in the price level and the prevention of excessive growth in external debt. These objectives have, however, specific role in stablization program depending on the weight each objective bears in each developing country. In recent years the fiscal policy in stabilization programs has started to emphasize the structural elements of the stabilization programs design include incentive measures implemented through the exchange rate, import liberalization, financial deregulation, pricing policy etc. There are also controls where institutional bottlenecks exist or these institutions are not fairly developed. In such a situation the fiscal policy is considered as a major instrument for attainment of economic development with stability which often is beset with shortcomings in administrative structure or pressures developed in the political horizon of external shocks.

Furthermore, tax evasion, rising price level together with pressures developed through the political grouping of the parliamentary opposition and weak monitoring system of the Government expenditure have undermined the strength of the fiscal policy as a stabilization force and it has instead contributed to the disequilibria or imbalance in the funding institutions, like the IMF in negotiating stabilization programs. During the 1970's the increase in the oil price created a new environment which complicated the international financing mechanism. As a consequence of this, many countries have been compelled to pursue programs of stabilization policies with the objective of reducing external imbalances as well as the rate of inflation. These policies have often been contrary to the growth process. The republic of Korea succeeded in stabilizing their economy even in the face of external shocks while others were less success-ful. Further, some countries experienced short-term political costs of the stabilization policies extended over a long period rather than the long run economic benefits. As the stabilization policies were inhibiting, growth became apparent and the Government policy makers concentrated attention on growth rather than the stabilization irrespective of the consequences for the balance of payments and the rate of inflation. They accepted the position that inflation is a lesser evil than stagnation and that the external sector can be kept in equilibrium by means of quantitative re-strictions and export subsidies or repudiating exter-nal debt obligations.

Stabilization and growth have been the policy objec-tives although the emphasis at a particular point of time may be placed on one instead of the two togeth-er although the two objectives are inseparable. The stabilization programs must give adequate emphasis on growth in order to ensure that the stability is not achieved at the cost of stagnation causing difficulties in reducing over a time the burden of debt. A general conclusion is that achieving growth without stability is both technically and politically impossible either in the short run or in the long run. It is, therefore, essential to reformulate the stabilization program or policies that would give emphasis to incorporate a fiscal design in order to achieve specific targets in the growth objective.

The traditional demand management policies can work well in case of the stabilization policy as the only objective of economic policies. However, in the case of the stabilization with growth the demand management policies need to be complimented by policies aimed at increasing potential output. To achieve this, the structural policies need to be well guided and well planned so that the potential output increases through proper allocation of resources and increasing the growth rates of the factors of production. Lack of well-designed structural policies have been the main cause of stagnation and instability in the economic system. Therefore, any design of adjustment programs must either integrate the policy of stabilization with growth or demand management policies with structural policies in the supply side. Stabilization program may indicate either specific or general fiscal policies under which a member country of the IMF may agree with the latter either in part or a whole range of specific fiscal measures i.e., changes in various taxes and changes in specific public expenditures, subsidies and public utility rates. These measures taken together would add up to the required adjustment in aggregate demand and supply so as to reduce the balance of payments disequilibrium and the rate of inflation to the desired levels. This is the macro-economic approach to the stabilization programs.

An alternative approach is related to the size of the fiscal deficit and to the expansion of bank credit emanating from the financing of the deficit. Specific policies in regards to the macro-economic variables would be to assess their immediate impact on the size of the fiscal deficit and on aggregate demand.

In recent years stabilization programs established fiscal ceilings on the basis of the implicit model connected with monetary expansion associated with fiscal deficit to development in the balance of payments. Now the countries will need to choose the specific ways in which the fiscal ceiling would be observed. The authorities need to determine which tax rates and revenue measures need to be changed and which expenditures should be reduced or increased.

The IMF mission provide advice on technical assistance reports. Performance criteria must be confined to macro-economic variables. The concept of macroeconomic variables involves the idea of aggregation and includes the broadest possible aggregate in an economic category. While the fund may not necessarily be involved in the detailed decision by which general policies are put into operation the general conclusion is that specific prices of commodities or services, specific taxes or other detailed measures to increase revenues or to reduce expenditures are not to be considered as macroeconomic variables. In the stabilization program the observance of the fiscal ceilings has been the most essential element.

As a leading financial institution IMF has provided advice on tax structure, structure of public spending and their administration through its technical assistance program. Specific advice has been provided to the countries on how to raise revenue keeping in view the macro-economic approach to stabilization programs. Starting with the macro-economic approach to stabilization programs the Fund mission began paying more attention to structural aspects in general and specific fiscal aspects in particular.

In negotiating stabilization programs the approach begins with an estimation of the required reduction in the fiscal deficit of a country given its balance of payments position and availability of foreign financing. In the medium term the connection that exists between the deficit reduction and the specific measures to make the reduction possible is not accounted for in setting program ceilings.

The removal of growth retarding taxes is not encouraged if alternative sources of revenue are not immediately available. Because such a removal of taxes will immediately increase the fiscal deficit leading to deterioration in the countries' external position. Thus, the approach of the Fund is from macro-economic to micro-economic considerations paying more attention to the size of the fiscal deficit and it's financing. The argument put forward for macro-economic approach is objective at least theoretically as under this approach the authorities know that they will obtain the agreed financial support from the Fund if the country satisfies the performance criteria related to macro-economic variables. The performance criteria based on ceilings meet the approval of the parliament as it implies less interference by the Fund in the internal affairs of countries than do the criteria related to specific measures. Performance criteria are also objective in the sense that a member country will riot have the chance to object to the changed decision of the Fund at any time to impede transactions under the standby arrangement. The member has maximum assurance about the circumstances in which it can engage in transactions with the Fund. Some programs have made the total level of public expenditure a performance clause which is considered as narrow interpretation of conditionality guidelines. However, all formal agreements have, in general, focused on the difference between public expenditure and revenue (i.e. on the deficit).

The usual formulation of a stabilization program may give the impression that the relationship between fiscal deficits and program objective and their relationship with the balance of payments is clear cut and unambiguous. It may give the impression of a single valued functional relationship i.e. so much fiscal deficit implies so much deficit in the current account of the balance of payments. Knowledge about important economic relationship, such as, between changes in prices, changes in nominal exchange rates and their effects on balance of payment is too limited to inspire confidence about the precise level of the fiscal deficit required to achieve a given change in the current account of the balance of payments or in other economic objectives.

The ceilings may, in some cases, divert attention away from basic objectives of economic policy. Programs may be judged successful or not depending on whether ceilings are being met rather than on whether the ultimate objectives of the programs i.e., durable improvement in the balance of payments, growth, price stability are being achieved.

Finally, excessive reliance on macro-economic ceilings may divert attention away from quality as well as the durability of the specific measures used by a country to comply with its performance clauses. As to the durability of the fiscal measure the question to be raised is the following:

- will a fiscal measure have permanent impact on the fiscal deficit?
- will a revenue increase or an expenditure cut for years to come or will have once for all effect?

This is an important question if the program's objective should bring about a permanent improvement in the economy. There are instances of advance payments of tax by enterprises at the request of the Government or public expenditure has been postponed through the building up of arrears or the postponement of inevitable expenditures so that the country can make the fiscal ceilings and make the next drawing. In other cases, temporary sources of revenue - once for all taxes, temporary surcharges, tax amnesties, sale of public assets etc. have allowed the country to stay within the agreed ceiling without doing anything to reduce its underlying or core fiscal deficit. In addition to the question of durability of the fiscal measures there is the important question of the quality i.e., economic efficiency of the measure.

STABILIZATION POLICY AND ECONOMIC GROWTH

Stabilization policy that promotes growth requires that the reduction in the fiscal deficit be carried out through fiscal measures that are durable as well as efficient in their effects. The policies chosen must not be self-destructive once the program is over and must achieve their deficit reducing objective with at least possible inhibition of economic growth. Recent work has demonstrated that the efficiency of fiscal instruments is important for growth – work effort, exports, productive investment, savings, capital flight, foreign investment and so on can be effected by the choice of specific fiscal instruments. These fiscal choices will determine the amount of foreign resources that may be available for a country during and after a program period. Thus, the basic conclusion is that the relationship between the size of the fiscal deficit and changes in the alternative objectives of economic policy i.e., growth and stability is significantly influenced by the fiscal measures implemented, the latter can make a substantial difference to the growth prospects of a country, if the fiscal deficit is reduced by eliminating a totally unproductive expenditure or by raising a tax that has strong disincentive effects.

Thus, the more efficient the measure used to achieve a given deficit reduction the greater will be the rate of growth. Provided the monetary policy remains unchanged the rate of inflation will be lower. For stabilization programs provided that a country is willing to implement considerable structural measures in the early stage of program period so that the positive effects of these measures can be felt relatively in the early stage, the Fund may, then require less reduction in the overall deficit i.e., to require less austerity than the situation when the structural packages are less far reaching in the case of its delayed introduction and implementation.

Thus, what is important for the Fund in entering into an agreement with a country is a trade-off, between quantity and quality of fiscal adjustment when this is influenced by the timing of the introduction of the structural measures.

The Fund has attempted to ensure that cutback in Government expenditure are focused on less productive activities. The expenditure policies pursued have in several instances, not been as supportive of the growth objective as they could have been.

Considerations in cutback in expenditure have not necessarily on economic efficiency but more on political considerations. An examination in cutback in capital expenditure in various countries have indicated that they have often borne by some more productive projects. In order to reduce the budget deficit the cutback in some cases affected productive externally financed projects, despite the fact that the loans for part of the total cost of the projects were highly concessionary.

In some other cases, the cutbacks have focused on productive domestically financed small scale projects while externally financed highly visible but less productive projects backed by important donors have been protected.

In some other cases when a core investment programme has been agreed between the country and the World Bank higher implementation rates for lower priority projects have occurred. Such policies have a common feature being the disproportionate cutback in expenditure on materials, supplies and maintenance relative to other types of expenditure resulting in deterioration of the condition of roads, bridges, public buildings, irrigation projects, airports and other public sector building notwithstanding the inevitability of certain adjustments necessitated by the debt crisis. These expenditures are generally classified by current rather than capital expenditures.

As such the common view that stabilization programs must protect investment may not necessarily lead to the best policy in cases where the most productive expenditures are current ones. There is a growing concern among some experts that present reductions in fiscal deficits associated with these lower expenditures for maintenance of roads and other infrastructure will necessitate much higher expenditure and thus higher deficits in future years which is just the shifting of the fiscal deficit from the present to the future.

On the other hand, tax increases in some cases, included measures that proved to be detrimental to the growth of the economy. This particularly happened in countries with very high tax ratios. On many occasions, the rates of export duty have been imposed following devaluation on the grounds that the exporters enjoy some sort of windfall profits, while devaluation often offset past cost increases, import surcharges have been levied or the rates of import duty have been raised for balance of payments purpose and for revenue increase. Sometimes these taxes have been imposed on certain products which are already highly taxed and thus increasing the differences in the tax rates between taxed and untaxed imports thereby increasing further distortions and reducing the prospects for growth of the economy. In many developing countries the imports subjected to import duty are often less than 50 per cent of total imports, so that substantial rate increases on the taxed imports are needed to generate significant amount of revenue from this source. These increases in rates result in further smuggling causing further loss of revenue.

The impact of changes in fiscal deficits on the development activities depended, to a considerable extent on the quality of measures adopted both in the revenue side and the expenditure side of the budget. A change in the quality of these measures will change the relationship between the fiscal deficit and the balance of payments over the medium and long-term.

The reduction in the fiscal deficit through austerity measures needed to achieve a given effect on the basic objectives of economic policy will be more severe as less efficient measures are chosen. Any stabilization programs should, therefore, deal with in a more objective manner the macro-economic issues of public finance in addition to other structural policies in the socio-economic front. Such programs must include needed structural changes in the overall economic system and must integrate them with the macro-economic framework.

CHAPTER 6

Strengthening of Institutional Capacity for Poverty Reduction in Poor Countries

For improving lives of the millions of people through new types of development work what is necessary is strengthening of institutional capacity. But, unfortunately, this approach for capacity development for bringing about tangible benefits to the poverty stricken people is lacking in many ways in most of the countries of the south Asia and around the world. A recent estimate says about 1.2 billion people still just live on less than one dollar a day, while almost 859 million people go hungry almost every night. The root of the problem is not about how much wealth one has acquired or money one has earned, the real problem is the lack of access to essential sources to lead an affluent, carefree but hazardless life which go beyond financial stringency affecting peoples' health, education, security and opportunities for participation in political affairs or debates either local or national. The solutions for endemic poverty will also have to address the poverty impact on women mostly originated from local environmental factors and situations that continued for ages necessitating enhancement of local capacity to respond to new challenges to work for women development.

No doubt economic growth is essential for lifting people out of poverty trap but this is not enough. The institutions entrusted with the task of carrying out development work program need to be strengthened to empower the citizens they serve. The financial and technical assistance program of the donor agencies the mainstay of poverty prescriptions has often resulted in bigger challenges to growth that require long term incremental responses of the community. This prominently requires that solutions for poverty prescriptions should be designed in such a way that fits well into the overall strategy of political, organizational or capacity change of the society.

A network of development observatories is one way of setting up a system for gathering quantitative and qualitative data related to the national poverty reduction strategy. Under such a project local municipal authorities can be trained in the use and interpretation of statistical data. With the compilation and analysis of such statistical information a bridge between local researchers and local authorities is established to outreach to communities for sharing knowledge by engaging the public for anti-poverty solutions. Such a project apart from making poverty reduction strategies is more responsive to the needs and demands of those most affected and increasing public responses for public prescription. The advantages of public prescription through grassroots research at local levels is that a reliable data base of resources is created automatically so that the authority can be assured of the available experts, program activities and required investments that can be consulted mutually and shared nation-wide. Such statistical information can be gathered through a household survey. This kind of observatory system using the MDGs in addition to the existing poverty reduction strategy may be put in practice as research platform in many countries of the Southeast Asia and other smaller countries of Asia and the Pacific. By 2006, the forest regions of Guinea, historically the countries bread basket was suffering the repercussions of conflicts in neighbouring Cote d'Ivoire, Liberia and Sierra Leone. More than 45,000 refugees, internally displaced persons had flooded the region stretching basic social services beyond capacity putting human development in a precarious situation. What the Government did was that in 2007 the Government partnered with the UN system and others to devise a long term intervention strategy to address the needs of the affected population aiming at improving local capacity in the area of food security, HIV response, basic social provisions and governance. The result was that the program has helped 3,250 households to improve agricultural output providing training in production techniques to 50 community groups comprising over 3,000 members. The program also introduced a community based approach to prevent the spread of HIV that led to 300 home visits and better targeted care for over 1000 orphans.

With this awareness raising campaign around water borne diseases, over 2600 water sources have been disinfected impacting 148 villages throughout the region. Educational opportunities have improved under the program with over 15,000 people, 65 per cent of them are female enrolled in training or literacy programs and 43 new classrooms built.

The education targets contained in the MDGs have prompted not only an increase in primary school enrolment but also a renewed emphasis on secondary education and tertiary education opportunities as capacity development strategies move upstream. There are examples where international organizations like UNDP helped countries to narrow national and regional disparities in secondary enrolment through an e-School Program. The Project has succeeded in equipping every high school in many countries with a computer laboratory establishing a national Information and Communications Technology (ICT) curriculum for schools and creating a training and certification program for ICT to a large number of high school and college students in many countries.

In many countries micro-finance as a single mechanism has been serving as multiple capacity development goals. In Syria UNDP supported poor north-eastern project to promote local development and empower vulnerable groups through micro-finance and set up a network of 32 village Development Funds in over 40 villages to administer micro loans over the short-term with the longer goal of developing and sustaining micro-finance institutions to serve the area. The project by making loan disbursements to over 7,800 households, served the area by raising their incomes by 20 per cent. Nearly half of the borrowers were women accounting for 46 per cent of the 1,000 jobs created as a result of the initiative. 25 adult literacy programs have been set up throughout the area along with two kindergartens allowing women to attend classes while their children are being cared for. This kind of initiative has created a socio-economic data base to track progress in the region in key areas including population growth, household size, size of livestock, amount and percentage of arable land, and literacy rates. As people were thus inspired by these initiatives in the country a decree has been passed allowing for establishment of additional micro-finance institutions.

Already the UN Capital Development Fund (UNCDF) and UNDP have their combined mandate for joint work on local development through local authorities in the Least Developed Countries (LDCs) to build capacity of and to provide investment resources to local

Governments in the form of investment capital for block grants, capacity development support and technical advisory services. All these need to be monitored so essential for piloting innovations in capacity development that, when these are successful, can be scaled up by national Governments and integrated in their respective development programs and replicated in other countries as well facing similar challenges. Many less developed countries are facing the challenges of defining and implementing decentralization reforms and to enhance the effectiveness and to promote local Governments with the sole purpose of alleviating poverty at the grass root level. The Decentralization and local Government support program is to improve the decentralized system in many countries to strengthen local institutional capacities in public expenditure management program. Such a Program in many countries involves the use of mobile capacity development teams with regionally based experts seconded from different ministry offices that are mobilized to bring their practical knowledge to local authorities and to share best practices to maintain development balance between regions.

What is pertinent issue here in development is to face the challenge of alleviating poverty either through national Governments or international aid agencies as an opportunity to innovate and build on models that have proven successful in many countries making creative use of existing local resources. Mobile teams working in some countries specialize in a wide range of local skills development and expertise including participatory data collection, integrated planning, budget procurement, supervision of project implementation, accounting and reporting. This approach of development through mobile system facilitates the program of local development to build capacity where and when it is needed and in a manner that is responsive to the capacity requirements of an evolving local authority system. The scope of the program may then be extended and expanded over the whole region and integrated with the National Decentralization Strategy with a unified methodology and institutional framework for development.

CHAPTER 7

A Critical Role of the Fiscal Policy in the Perspective of Mobilization of Savings in Developing Countries

MOBILIZATION OF SAVINGS - GOVERNMENT POLICY

While mobilizing savings for growth it is essential for the policy makers to determine first the quantum of savings that may be channelled into the financial system for investment. Once the resources flow into the financial market it becomes necessary to determine how the system may operate effectively and efficiently in directing these resources to the sectors to meet the priority needs of the economy. Thus, by affecting the supply side i.e., savings or the demand side i.e., domestic investment, the Government may attempt to mobilize resources.

The Government policy in regard to the mobilization of resources may ensure that a significant portion of savings is directed toward the financial system. Thus, given this "Loanable funds savings", the Government may wish to overcome imperfections or distortions in the capital market which prevent investors from using these funds that may yleld the highest rate of return; or, raise the potential rates of return attainable by savers itself engaging in capital expenditures mainly on infrastructure and public goods which generate no immediate pecuniary profit but which increases the effectiveness of private projects and thus the demand for loan able funds to finance them. Thus, the roles of the Government may be characterized as entailing the removal of negative externalities distorting the social return to capital and enhancing positive externalities increasing the social return to capital. This role of the Government is based on the assumption that private capital markets are not perfect.

If the capital markets were developed then there would be no distortion in the supply side of or in demand side for loanable funds. On the supply side, the socially optimum level of savings and its allocation between markets would already exist. In this situation, the intervention of the Government to change either aggregate savings or its composition would lower long run economic welfare.

On the demand side, rates of return to capital would provide the correct signals to investors and market arbitrage would internalize the external benefits or costs to investment. The Government's role in mobilizing domestic financial resources will be more crucial in developing countries when the private sector's performance in generating and allocating loan able funds is insignificant.

Developing Country Financial Markets – Basic Characteristics

The characteristics of developing country capital markets indicate that savings are low and comprise mostly the non-loan able funds that are not available for investment in the purchase of new shares or creation of new capital. Wealth is generally held in these countries in the form of consumer durables, buying land or housing i.e., such forms of savings / investment that indirectly generate output or holding financial assets outside the formal financial system i.e., in informal "curb" markets. The size of the capital market being small the scope for diversification of financial institutions and financial instruments or assets is limited. The equity market is rarely developed investments in physical capital are few relative to the total size of the financial capital market. Consequently, there exists a wide differential in the rates of interest offered on different loans. Poor communications prevent the flow of information and advertising of the quantities and the prices of funds available. Pooling funds become difficult. The Government here cannot, for obvious

reasons, bid for funds. Further, the Government's clearly defined sectoral priorities are expressed through a
conscious policy of making different quantities available at different interest rates to different demanders
resulting in the markets' inability to generate a single
clearing rate of return to financial capital. Borrowing
and lending rates may lead to such anomalies as an individual saver finding that banking his savings is not
worthwhile but, on the other hand the borrowing to
support a planned enterprise may be too expensive.
This situation leads to increased use of retained earnings of investment in developing countries compared
to the situation in which financial intermediation is
developed. Financial returns to savings and or investments are insufficient. The wide discrepancies between the borrowing and lending rates make returns
in the financial system unattractive for two reasons:

1. Controls and intervention are widespread in
   many developing countries. For example, interest rate policies quickly lead to financial repression as foreign interest rate change, exchange

rates move up or the inflation rate rises. In these circumstances even if the capital market is characterized by complete information and open access, savings would fall short of the investment and necessitate retaining of the loanable funds the prices would then be prevented from functioning on allocative mechanism.

2. In less urbanized areas of some developing countries non-financial assets may serve as currency substitutes raising their liquidity premium compared to what the bankers would provide. The rate of return to financial assets might be higher outside cities. This renders the financial sector to measure the opportunity cost of alternative assets and offer competitive rates of return.

The liquidity of financial assets may not be guaranteed in many developing countries due to frequent changes of Government policy in regard to the change of interest rates, retirement of bonds and altering the purchasing power of the currency. These changes are often the result of unavoidable exogenous shocks which may not affect the stability of the financial system but may cause the costs of imports and exports to fluctuate widely.

DOMESTIC FINANCIAL MARKETS AND THE ROLE OF THE GOVERNMENT

It is through the taxes or the credit policy that the distortions in the financial markets can be removed through the adjustment of the incentives to holdings financial assets. However, the Government may not have complete information on the rate of return which would compensate people for the cost of storing savings in a faraway city. In a larger capital market, sufficient numbers of transactions would take place for the clearing rate of return to manifest itself while in developing countries, because the capital is so small so that the Government in order for the incentives to be appropriate, it has to set the level of these incentives without receiving signals from the market. In the informal market in the absence of the market clearing price it might at least try to encourage savings and investment by increasing returns through tax policy either broad or selective incentives or through the credit policy that would favor certain projects.

TAX POLICIES AND MOBILIZATIONS OF SAVINGS

Tax policies to mobilize savings are intended to work by increasing the return to future consumption either to savings in general or savings held in specific form. There are tax systems under which savings are taxed twice, first when total income is taxed either it is consumed or saved or when savings generate interest. If this discrimination is lifted or lessened total savings would increase.

However, the scope for increasing savings in this way extends as far as the extreme case where only expenditure is taxed. In the same way, if the penalty for savings were lighter on some form of assets than others, people would tend to shift into those assets. The policy recommendations is to convert present income taxes into personal taxes on· consumption expenditure or into value added tax on the basis of consumption or highly specific tax incentives, such as, altering the tax treatment of social security contributions. It is notable that broad based incentives have not been widely used in many countries.

Many countries exempt interest income derived from certain assets or institutions. Some countries exempt all dividend income while some countries' tax policies favor retained earnings. Interest on various types of bank deposits is exempt from taxation in Argentina, Guatemala, Iran, the Republic of Korea, Malta, Panama and Paraguay. Financial company and or Investment Company is exempt in Argentina, Cyprus, and the Netherlands. Governments try to increase non-Government financing by exempting interest and gains from Government securities. There are other specific savings incentives, such as, Brazil requires employees to put 8 per cent employees' salaries into untaxed bank accounts in the names of the employees.

Micro-economic Consequences of Tax Incentives

Even if a change in tax policy would increase welfare by reducing discrimination against capital accumulation it does not follow that its adoption would result in more saving. A reduction in the return to saving through a capital income tax has both an income effect and a substitution effect. The increase in the relative cost of saving makes individuals prefer present consumption to saving and therefore, to future consumption. If the individual desires to spread his consumption evenly over his life time he will have to maintain a higher level of saving in light of the increased cost of saving than he would otherwise have chosen. He may find he has to save more than he did before in order to maintain a stable consumption pattern. As the rate of interest falls the present value of future earnings rises because it becomes more costly to substitute savings out of present income for future income in order of sustain future consumption. Thus, life time income i.e., present and future earnings rises somewhat to offset the reduction in the distortion caused by the income effect.

A reduction in the distortion caused by the tax will have an ambiguous result. We cannot tell whether capital income taxes will decrease or increase saving, therefore it is difficult to say precisely whether the removal of that distortion will move people into saving or out of saving because, given the higher return to saving they need to save less than before just to maintain the level of consumption that they planned for the rest of their lives.

Distortions Created by Tax Incentives

Tax incentives to save do generate a large response in the quantity of savings but this should not necessarily be followed as policy instrument by the Government to increase aggregate financial savings. The distortions inherent in them might be less detrimental to economic welfare than heavier taxes. Any tax on savings distorts the choice between present and future consumption. However, the distortions are worsened when different types of savings are taxed at different rates. This is because if after tax rates of return are equalized across different types of savings the given non-uniform tax rates the pre-tax return to each type of asset must be different. Thus distorting the flow of funds to each type of asset.

If the Government wishes only to alter the level of savings a system of specific tax incentives having different tax rates may decease welfare more than a heavier but uniform tax system. Research reveals that in inflationary circumstances the effective tax rates will be much higher than the statutory rates and the lower the tax rate the smaller is the differential between the two rates.

Therefore, the greatest welfare gains from savings incentives come through offsetting the inflation induced boost in effective tax rates. There are two common characteristics of developing countries that would generally vitiate the effects of savings incentives:

1. inflation at the high rates - which is difficult to predict in developing countries; and
2. the tax incentives – which have to be announced in advance as it gives a large margin for error favoring either the investors or the Government.

A common characteristic in developing countries is that the real rate of interest is either low or negative so that there is always a short supply of loanable funds and that investment is constrained by rationing of finance. Interest rates are not free to rise with inflation the effective tax rate is not boosted by inflation as it would happen. in a free market economy. Therefore, there is no increased distortion from the effect of the inflation component of the interest rate so that a reduction in tax a rates on the nominal interest rate could offset. Thus, in financially repressed economy the inflation argument in favor of tax incentives for saving is not valid. The fact that the interest income is subject to income tax may distort the saving decision of the people but this distortion may not be larger than the financial repression. Under the fixed interest rate ceiling the financial repression increases as the inflation increases. Thus, a Government wishing to increase saving would find it more appropriate to use the tax policy to prevent inflation instead of trying to offset inflation indirectly by using incentives which have the effect of indexing some selected returns to inflation. It can be emphasized that neither the theory of savings behavior nor the empirical evidence on the response of savings to changes in its rate of return support the use of tax incentives as an instrument to increase financial savings. Further, tax incentives may create economic distortions leaving the economy worse off than it would be under the distortions of a uniform tax system.

Tax Incentives and Macro-Economic Consequences

What is necessary is to obtain a comprehensive evaluation of the results of using incentive policies to promote aggregate saving and investment in the economy. In most cases tax incentives mean loss of potential fiscal revenues having direct budgetary implications. This loss of revenue will require either an increase in some other source of revenue or cut Government expenditure in certain sectors. Failure to take action will result in budgetary gap requiring additional financial resources. Thus, the implementation of a policy granting tax incentives may result either the need to increase other taxes and or reduce Government expenditure.

A program of tax incentives will result in budget imbalance if no measures are taken to compensate for the loss of revenue. The effects of which can only be assessed if information about the financing of such imbalances can be obtained. The fiscal deficits tend to put pressure. on aggregate demand resulting in higher inflation and balance of payments disequilibrium.

Further, if the deficits are debt financed, this will result in higher real interest rate and the crowding out of the private sector. With all these, it is inevitable that these will have detrimental effects on the savings and investment process. If tax incentives ultimately lead to acceleration in the inflationary process, then this outcome may cancel the benefits to the private sector largely. Such an environment will not be conducive to dynamic and sustained growth of saving and investment. A uniform tax associated with prudent macro-economic management may make higher rates more acceptable than under a tax system with many exemptions. This is again a fiscal position unsustainable in the long run. Surveys carried out in many developing countries have shown that lack of foreign investment and inability of many enterprises and individuals to obtain credit are serious obstacles to development.

What is essential for the Government policy implementation is to pursue policy for a sound and balanced macro-economic, management to provide a pool of funds savings to meet the investment needs of the public and private sectors.

CHAPTER 8

Global Economic Growth, Debt Relief and Investment in the Emerging Markets

E ssential role that trade growth plays in continued global economic growth and prosperity emphasize the need to overcome the serious obstacles to
trade among countries. Key players in all trade negotiations are to emphasize and required to take steps to

provide political impetus in order to bring the negotiations and turn them into an ambitious but comprehensive and successful development oriented projects for trade growth. If the negotiations fail or there is a breakdown, these will certainly bring about serious but long term adverse consequences to the poorest and most vulnerable countries of the East and the West.

Although strong growth in developing countries in recent years have brought about prospects for global economic growth both for high income and for low income developing countries some downside risks to this central prospect cannot be ignored. Major imbalances in the global economy, such as, rising inflation and interest rates while slowing down global growth will retard the flow of private investment in developing poor countries. In these circumstances it is most unlikely that these countries should be able to meet the MDGs. Besides, persistent higher oil price are causing income losses and putting strain in budgetary resources in many countries especially the oil importing countries.

POLICY COORDINATION

What is necessary in these circumstances is to face boldly and take concrete steps for a viable international coordination in policies to be pursued by individual countries. These policies relate to fiscal policies in the developed countries, structural reforms and some tighter policies on demand management in Southeast Asia and oil exporting countries together with maintaining foreign exchange stability. IMF as an international financial institution must continue to promote comprehensively its basic role in monetary management and balance of payment including surveillance of the exchange rates of the member countries with much greater force in policy coordination. The development partners will need to deliver on pledges to the poorest and vulnerable countries especially to those affected by trade shocks with much greater emphasis to mobilize financial resources, to help poor oil importing countries to mitigate the loss of income as a result of rising oil prices. An urgent need is also the recognition of the cost of adjustment in some countries facing serious erosion of trade preferences through commitment of aid resources to the countries hit by large trade shocks. These should be accompanied by measures facilitating lowering of trade barriers and thus sustaining benefit through freer trade for low income countries.

Specific policies for ·growth and livelihoods are the priority needs of the countries for which economic policies must go alongside the geography and institutional factors of the countries to bring about sustained growth of livelihoods. What the industrial countries can do is to strengthen the development dimension of the global trading system and reinforce the capacity of the international financial system specially directed towards solving the basic needs of the poor community. A stronger and viable growth policy on the key areas including the energy policies, comparatively liberal policy of migration, politically feasible international commitments of foreign assistance to provide effective programs of development in the new emerging countries should provide necessary impetus to the growth of trade and its dimension.

Of greater importance is the integration of education and micro level training with the strategic programme of growth and livelihoods in these poor countries for which the developed nations need to respond urgently to the long-term finance. A viable and innovative contribution of the civil society through their involvement in the formulation and implementation of national development projects is the need of the hour so much so that the resources are directed towards supporting the sectors of basic livelihoods of the rural and urban informal sub sectors including essential investment of roads, electricity, water supply and sanitation and other MDGs related investments. The developing poor countries business forums need to closely collaborate to work with the private sector to provide access to the increasing proportion of the population and enhance corporate governance.

DEBT RELIEF

Earlier IMF, International Development Association (IDA) and the African Development Fund (ADF) reached an agreement to implement the proposals for debt cancellation set out in Multilateral Debt Reduction Initiative (MDRI) the small states at the G8 summit that provides an escape for those countries that are eligible from the burden of debt accumulation. The summit emphasized that the donors should undertake to ensure that payments made to finance the reduction in debt are additional to their committed aid flow. It was agreed that any re accumulation of debt be managed carefully by the countries benefiting from this reduction (MDRI). In this connection joint IMF and World Bank framework for debt sustainability as well as the contribution made by the commonwealth secretariat to The Heavily Indebted Poor Countries (HIPC) on their commercially negotiated debts is a welcome step in this direction. In the similar way the international community needs to give attention to the debt burden of other poor countries specifically excluded from the MDRI but they have continued to service their debt notwithstanding the fact that domestic and foreign debt is imposing an unsustainable fiscal burden on these poor countries.

PRIVATE INVESTMENT FLOWS IN THE EMERGING MARKETS

To promote private investment into the emerging markets the commonwealth secretariat through the Commonwealth Private Investment Initiative (CPII) has continued their program in various regions of the member countries on SME sector in a wider range of developing countries.

The World Bank/Commonwealth Secretariat Joint Task Force have identified the dimensions of vulnerability of small states which still persist with new factors increasing vulnerability, faster than anticipated loss of trade preference, a rapidly growing debt burden in many small states, increasing environmental risks, rising concern of youth unemployment and crime including the HIV/AIDS. While tackling these challenges, the small states will need to take action to stabilize and diversify their economies, the international community will need to take stronger and more effective action to help small states address their problems including the adjustment cost associated with the loss of trade preferences combined with the specific policy and institutional prescriptions suited to the individual country circumstances.

The work program of the World Bank, the Commonwealth Secretariat and other development partners will need to be coordinated for implementing a road map of action for the small states. Since small states are susceptible to disasters it is urgently necessary that the heads of developed countries accord priority for a Catastrophe Risk Insurance Facility for the countries of the Pacific and the Caribbean.

Finally, a bridge between business and Government, between developed and emerging markets and between large and small businesses is the only way to expand business and investment by strengthening private sector linkages among the countries of the East and the West and in this private sector can come forward with their innovative ideas and recommendations for fostering a common platform for global public and private sector development.

CHAPTER 9

Ethics in Banks for Healthy
Financial Business

Ethical issue is of paramount importance in our national endeavour for self-sustaining growth of the economy through a reconstruction of the banking model particularly in the age of globalization, sophisticated management and electronic transfer of finance either nationally or internationally and relatively regulation free flow of resources across the borders. This situation is now rooted in our financial system in such a way that has given rise to inefficiency and total neglect of the vast mass of people at the grassroots level.

The countries of the Southeast Asia and some of the developing countries are now facing a great challenge in banking sector who are now subjected to overly delayed structural-transformation and scrutiny. Two opposing parties - one, the bank officials, directors and loan takers and the other, the depositors whose resources are deployed in the system and while their interest are being threatened.

In the past integrity was protected by simply adherence to rules and regulations and these were enough for ethical conduct and behavior in the banking business. But the situation has changed since then. Technology of fraudulent practices a common feature in these days of modern banking has worked towards making the banking system vulnerable to various shocks originating from the reckless misconduct by the people who are either the controllers at the policy levels/ directors or the managers at the operational level. This is so much a focal point in the banking arena that very often the influential loanees in conjunction with the people at the helm of affairs can jeopardize the policy functioning of the financial system comprised of the banks and financial institutions bringing serious repercussions in the economy.

In a dynamic world professional scrutiny for financial accommodation through evaluation and appraisal of projects is not always the rules of the game and very often supported by controllers and finance directors. This is how the ethical norms become challenging in banking and financial institutions. Hence the need for promoting ethics in the banking and non-banking financial institutions with strong commitment at the Government level for bringing the loan defaulters and offending bank officials to task. This would make the whole banking environment free from the undesirable pressures originating from the unions and allow the banking system to function within the legal framework that would be supportive of a professional banking model.

Banks as financial institutions work as intermediaries between savers of long term and short term funds mainly for transaction and precautionary purposes and 67 investors using these surplus funds to finance their trade and investment business. Because banks are increasingly coming forward to finance a variety of purposes investment. business is growing in importance as trade necessitating a careful balancing of costs and returns.

In a real situation, banks should normally perform useful functions to facilitate production and exchange. This intermediary function will be viable as long as several interests are served under the binds of professional ethics and limits of law and guidance of central authority leading to total protection of the interest of savers and borrowers and help optimization of the returns from their involvement and intermediation of the bank.

The way to avoid all kinds of unethical practices in banks is through transparent initiation, information processing and accountable decision making. Since legal framework for banks and financial institutions do not adequately provide for this dependence on the decision makers, supervisors, monitors and controllers become inevitable. As a result, the banks have failed to optimize their organizational and their national interest with professional devotion. They have not been able to maximize returns from use of finance deposited with them resorting to implicit bar gaining process by the influential clients and decision makers and other organized actors i.e., officials, unions within the system. As a result, there has been a complete absence of neutrality and efficiency promoting organizational ethics.

The growth of human and social capital that rein forces shared values and stimulates a society is the only way to attack the issue and establish an ethical standard in the banking system. The critical point at issue to be addressed is how the banks should operate in a system of anarchy and corrupt practices of the giant industrialists and the bankers nurtured in the western style system.

While the behavioral norms of bank officials, directors and loan takers are guided by the model unsuited to our system, the objectivity of the whole operations of the banking system is intended only to serve people having vested interest in their respective enterprises. This is a focal point which needs to be brought out in clear term for public debate. This fundamental issue by any means has disturbed the equilibrium in the system tending to a continued decline in ethical behavior and standard. An analysis in depth is necessary to unearth the hindrances and the behavioral pattern of the major creators of the disturbances responsible for creating panic in the economy.

Banks in Bangladesh have failed to generate resources in real terms from deployment of resources, deposited by the general public. This is mostly attributed to the inability of the banks to forecast changes the socioeconomic behavior and direct resources to resolve the issues detrimental to the collective interest of the people at different levels below the poverty line. On this account, the banks could neither improve nor recover from the unregulated organizational ethics. Herein lies the urgent need of breaking the present institutional environment towards a viable system in all its operational policies and programs for action. This vital institutional draw back of the present environment in banking business need to be focused and debated on the public front.

What we need is to go beyond stating that the bank is a socially productive organization. The sole expectation of the society and the country cannot be met without an independent and mutually re-enforcing strategies of sectoral operations with the ultimate objective of participatory economy which is the urgent call of the society.

Advocacy of Friedman for social responsibility of banking to use its resources in a way that would maximize the total 'product' and 'profitability' is not tenable in our society where moral and ethical values have now been relegated to secondary importance while deception and fraud are the rules of the game.

What is necessary is to change the whole system keeping moral considerations in the forefront through policy changes, attitude towards work through innovative ventures for upgrading the social values. The vital point at issue is that both banks and business houses must follow a definite path of the norms of justice, equity and fairness and only then the practices of fraud, bribery, hiding facts and often lying will diminish while a sense of honest practices will prevail to eliminate all unethical conduct of business in the banking sector.

The crux of the unhealthy situation that is now obtaining in the banking behavior is rooted in the exercise of discretion and discrimination so rampant in the business of both making advance and loans to the parties as well as in the management of personnel. This points to the need to uproot the basic malaise in banking business for which banking executives must adhere to the norms of fairness, equity and justice and that they must not engage in unfair activities on their own part or under pressure from any group. This is a trend of activities in the banking and finance sector in many developing countries and these have multiplied often inadequately denounced by business managers, business associations, policy makers and academics at large.

While business in general and banking in particular have to base their activities on trust, any discrimination and inconsistent norms obviously strike at the very root of this trust. These standpoints in the banking business need to be tested and applied in the process of recruitment, planning and incentives in all banking services that will require fairness, justice in order to promote consistency, accountability in the banking domain.

An overall conclusion that emerges from the above is how to promote and maintain an ethical standard in the interest of smooth functioning of banking institutions free from punishment and all sorts of societal pressure exerted. What is most apparent is lack of strong will that is mostly confronted by weakness of will for the fear of punishment that is often compounded by cumbersome legal process.

In this context we need to devise effective ways of developing ethical principles in all banking business through developing code of ethics and essential rules to be distinctly followed. There is a strong need for co-ordination of the codes of ethics to be followed by the

Chambers of trade associations of business and banking sector professional in order to assist and make the individuals duty bound to change their behaviroral pattern. Here the Chambers of trade and business associations in conjunction with the banks and financial institutions have a specific role to play in developing codes of ethics and should jointly go in for effective monitoring of ethical norms set forth in the guidelines. Similarly, the banks on their part should develop specific codes of ethics for its various professionals and devise ways to carefully monitor them on day-to-day basis. These codes of ethics will ultimately indicate the social and moral responsibilities of the bank staff at different levels and ensure strict compliance with perceptible impact in the banking environment. These codes of conduct may in the first instance be very difficult to enforce in the given circumstances but when these are brought to the eyes of the public the violators of these ethical norms may find themselves in sensitive position in respect of conducting them below the line.

What is the most unfortunate situation is the lack of transparency in the enforcement of the Government measures to update the rules and regulations taken to uproot the existing malpractices in the banks. It is only through the legislative an4 executive apparatus of the Government that such violation of ethical norms of the banks can be dealt with to protect the broad public interest as it is apparent that often the demands of social justice are in conflict with self-interest. Herein lies the strong necessity of enforcement of the rules from the top of the Government machinery.

From the above our conclusion is that the banks today must not concern themselves with only making profit while they can only exist if their main business is directed towards achieving the social goal of benefiting a wide spectrum of the society and the economy at large in terms of delivering social goods and services.

CHAPTER 10

Freeing up Trade for Alleviation
of Poverty

F reeing up trade is one of the most effective means in the step towards alleviation of poverty rather, to state it correctly, in the fight against poverty. But, unfortunately, the developing countries are deprived of reaping the benefits of trade as a result of prevalence of most unfair trade rules and practices. This can be explained in the most simple way how can a farmer in Cameroon barely earning US $400 a year on two hectares of land hope to compete with large American cotton producers who receive US $100,000 a year. The developing countries have been experiencing serious difficulties with so much of trade barriers and trade anomalies that they have been continuously advised as to the only way to prosperity is through pursuing a policy of trade liberalization. But then this is hardly possible unless many developed countries reciprocate the removal of trade barriers. While the fact is that those sectors where developing countries have a comparative advantage, such as, agriculture and textiles, developed countries have protected themselves through both tariff and non-tariff barriers and extensive systems of domestic subsidies resulting in developing exports. It is also a fact that Governments in the rich world the US, Europe and Japan spend US$ 1 billion a day supporting their own farmers at the expense of poor farmers in developing countries. But, with what result? The result is that the farmers in the US can sell their cotton at a lower price to the west African farmers even it costs them more to produce.

The above can be further exemplified with European Union (EU) subsidies and market restrictions costing Mozambique US $38 million and Malawi US $32 million. This is not only economically absurd but morally repugnant. In this continued trade apartheid what the developed countries can do is to give them access to their markets with all possible lines of credit and investment facilities.

As per estimate of the World Bank, the opening of markets by the rich countries alone can lift up to 144 million people out of poverty by 2015. Another estimate reveals the fact that after the Second World War, each citizen in Europe received the equivalent of US $220 under the Marshall Plan, whereas the African countries receive today from EU countries less than $10 per day per African citizen. This statistical information is heart breaking to those who work or think for humanitarian benefit and search for finding a way out in this moral degradation and equality of human rights. Therefore, realizing the fact that opening the markets of the developed countries to the developing poor countries and lowering of trade subsidies is the only means of alleviating poverty which in turn, act on serving the mutual benefit to all the beneficiaries. Let us think clearly on subsidy issues which is mutually beneficial to every trade partner. This is not to suggest that subsidies should be totally withdrawn but then this can be phased out to reduce real cost of products at the consumer's level. The Government's saving on subsidies can give advantages and yield better returns in terms of investment in social sectors like health, education and public services and then this can also result in lowering taxation of the common people.

Above is the gravity of the situation compounded by complex factors like, flow of investment, interest rate movement, trade and subsidy anomalies and a host of other factors in the developed world affecting the destiny of the developing poor countries. All global organizations need to give serious thought in their topmost agenda to root out the evils in the smooth functioning of development economics in the present day world economic situation.

Currently, the developing countries need to be compensated in monetary terms for the erosion of trade preference resulting from trade liberalization under the World Trade Organization (WTO) regime.

CHAPTER 11

Macro-Economic Performance and Challenges in Bangladesh

M acro-economic performance in Bangladesh needs to be judged and evaluated on the realities of economic events obtaining at a particular point of time and conducting evidence based research to address the issues. Successes, failures or mistakes of the Government policies at public and private sectors level pointing out the economic benefits which would otherwise have been achieved should be placed distinctly for public discussion.

Movement of major economic indicators, like, GDP, savings and investment, consumption public and private, on the one hand, movement of prices, wages and employment, on the other, will need to be examined in the context of policy variables and governance in conjunction with fiscal, monetary and financial sector development in the recent past. An evaluation of how these operational policy inputs of the Government, private sector, public and private sector enterprises have worked in major sectoral fields as these are reflected in the prioritized sectors, such as, poverty alleviation, human resources development and environmental development need consistent analysis and judgement for firming up realistic decisions in the management of future economic growth path. Any suggestive actions, for example, needed to accelerate investment, exports, and remittances to withstand the recessionary trend in the economy will have to be counteracted through deployment of Government policies in the internal and external front in the most effective manner and time bound programme. Any delay or hasty policy decision may create problems which the economy may not be able sustain in the long run. Government expenditure, for example, must be directed in the most productive and employment generation projects with periodic / frequent assessment of revenue in direct consultation with the ministries / agencies within the fiscal year in close coordination with monetary and credit policies of the banks and financial institutions so that any imbalance does not create any pressure on already mounting public debt and overall balance of payments (current and capital account) should be placed on high agenda. A comparative picture of economic, financial and non-financial sectors including those of social and infrastructure development sectors will largely indicate the state of development of the economy of Bangladesh.

A summary or an approximate view of the economy that centres around GDP movement or that of per capita income or savings and investment ratios often provide a cursory view of the economy without going deep into the working of the Government policies inside the real sectors of the economy.

In Bangladesh the most common sectors of measurement of macro-economic performance are the financial sector, external sector, food production and distribution sector and industrial sector covering large, small and medium industries sector which faced turbulent nature of growth after independence in 1972.

The Government's efforts to stimulate the economy through various incentive measures have often failed to generate the real strength, capability and potentiality of the economy's capacity for self-sustaining growth. There always exists a serious gap between household capacities and expanding economic growth and economic opportunities.

The fundamental reason is that there is a clear lack of consensus in setting national priorities of development work between the Government and the agencies either at home or abroad. Any program of work needs to be undertaken after due consultation with different stakeholders, such as, the private sector, civil society and non-Government organizations (NGOs).

There must be a good sense of participation between the Government and the development partners not simply by surrendering to the whims of the development partners. In light of the agreement reached between the Government and the Development partners at the recently concluded Bangladesh Development Forum to move ahead with 26 action plans aimed at improving governance and making more effective use of donor assistance is a welcome step. There has long been a gap of understanding and lack of open consensus between the donor agencies and the Government agencies' needs and problems related to the utilization of funds in various projects for which there has always been a growing amount of undisbursed funds without any effect on the economy's capacity to grow. The problem has always been a lack of proper planning and commitment to make the Government apparatus to work more smoothly and accountability.

An effective use of foreign assistance should help to ensure that all Government services are delivered in a more efficient manner and Government revenue realization improves. Indeed this kind of partnership and cooperation is long overdue will bring about real improvement in utilization of funds.

MAJOR POLICY ISSUES AND ACTIONS INFLATION

Inflation can emerge at any time in an economy as the most crucial challenge for a country like Bangladesh in maintaining macro-economic stability in the short and long run. To curb inflation it is necessary to ensure a higher domestic production of food grains mainly rice so that Bangladesh can narrow its reliance on food imports. It is reported that the country's food inflation reached as high as 10.56 per cent after 15 months against 12.02 per cent in 2008 while non-food inflation had shown slightly declining trend at 6.53 per cent. An overall inflation in January 2010 at 8.99 per cent should be a matter of concern for the policy makers that we remain at a comfortable level by end June, 2010. Whether this situation is due to impacts of price hikes on the international markets or due to increases in remittance flow and foreign currency reserves need to be corrected by unhindered supply of commodities and more efficient distribution. The Open Market Sale (OMS) and Vulnerable Group Feeding (VGF) programmes must work besides raising Boro rice production to ensure food supply. The challenging areas where investment needs to be revitalized are stimulation of the export sector through faster implementation of the stimulus package diversification of market and product as well as maintaining competitive exchange rate. Revenue collection enhancement and creation of employment opportunities under the bleak investment scenario are challenges for Bangladesh in attaining a 5.5 - 6.00 per cent growth in this fiscal.

The investment scenario needs to be significantly energized in near and medium term if GDP growth targets are to be achieved. Low inflation will be crucial in terms of translating macro-economic stability into higher GDP growth via accelerated investment.

What is needed at this hour is greater assistance from developed countries to the less developed countries for the economic advancement of such countries. A lack of adequate resources still remains as a key challenge for the Least Developed Countries (LDC) of the region including Bangladesh. The Brussels program of Action for the LDCs for 2001-2010 endorsed by the General Assembly represents a time bound comprehensive poverty reduction strategy with 30 internationally agreed development goals.

TRADE RELATIONS WITH INDIA

An urgent need of the hour is to develop trade relationship with the neighbouring country, India. It is estimated that Bangladesh stands to earn $ 1billion in transit fee if it allows free movement of Indian goods. If goods from north-east and other parts of India were to pass through Bangladesh it would fetch considerable transit revenue for Bangladesh besides cutting transportation time and cost for Indian goods. Bangladesh needs to identify new products for exports to Indian market and diversify its export particularly in non-traditional exports. While India's exports to Bangladesh is fairly diversified including agricultural commodities, manufactured items, heavy and medium machineries Bangladesh's exports are confined to only primary products. Bangladesh needs to widen its manufactured base in all sectors through research and development and transfer of technology and market based effective pricing system. Huge investment is required in increasing the productivity of Bangladesh's industrial sector and building its technical and technological capacity.

The recent signing of bilateral investment protection and promotion agreement would lead to greater investment in Bangladesh. In order to attract more investment from India it is necessary to open single window clearance for investment proposals, setting up an industrial park for India outside export processing zone with all infrastructure facilities, up gradation of tax holiday system.

At present there is severe infrastructural bottlenecks relating to power, ports, gas and telecommunication that push up quite significantly the cost of production, impede productivity growth and affect export competitiveness. In spite of these constraints a remarkable progress in macro-economic management has been achieved including acceleration of economic growth, gradual decline of budget deficit and high rate of export and import growth and a steady rise of foreign currency reserve.

The rate of inflation dropped to 6 per cent in September-October 2009 from 9.93 per cent in fiscal 2008. Simultaneously revenue GDP ratio stood at 10.92 per cent last fiscal year. The trend in revenue expenditure in the priority social sectors like human development, building rural. Infrastructure and poverty reduction has been increasing. A hike in the prices of food and fuel, and the global financial crisis are the major macro-economic challenges for Bangladesh.

The Government has also taken some reform measures to refurbish different sectors including the budgetary system, financial institutions and money markets and the revenue sector. A significant progress has now been attained in Millennium Development Goals (MDGs) including gender parity in primary and secondary education, enrolment in primary education and reduction in child mortality · rate. The rate of poverty has now declined from 58.8 per cent in 1991-92 to 48.9 per cent in 2000-2005. Improvement in the human development index has also been noticed with a ranking 146th out of 182 countries. The country now faces the challenges due to limited investible resources, uninterrupted corruption deteriorating law and order situation, exponential growth of population, malpractices in general administration and poor implementation capability of the people in charge of carrying out development projects, lack of transparency in public procurement and inadequate infrastructure.

Above all, institutional barriers hinder investment flow in South Asian Association for Regional Cooperation (SAARC) countries. These barriers are many non-tariff barriers, high cost of doing business, weak banking system and poor investment climate are hindering the investment flow from members of the regional forum.

Time has come to consolidate friendship to bring mutual economic benefit to the people of Bangladesh and the neighbouring countries. Recent visit of the Turkish president, for example, should be of immense value in terms of economic ties, economic security and stability. Turkey is looking forward to raising trade volume with Bangladesh to $ 1 billion. The bilateral trade rose to 409.14 million in fiscal 2008-2009 from below $ 100 million in 2003-2004 with Bangladesh enjoying a trade balance. Bangladesh exports to Turkey mainly include jute yarn and twine, knitwear and woven garments to the Eurasian country and imports are base metals, machinery and mechanical appliances and electrical equipment. At this juncture the two trade bodies of these two countries should exchange information on the state of their economies, commercial and economic legislation to further strengthen the ties. Various issues, such as, joint ventures, foreign direct investment and transfer of technologies should come up for discussion between the two parties. Technical support to the field of small and medium enterprises is another aspect of the two trade bodies that can extend bilateral collaboration.

A supportive monetary and credit policy aiming to increase investment in the most productive sectors and quick yielding projects that will create increasing resources for self-financing is the need of the hour. A constant watch will be needed to recover exports and new investments. To reach these goals the Government credit growth should be fairly high by June, 2010 compared to June, 2009 with a similar growth of credit to the private sector Prices of food and non-food commodities have shown an uptrend in the international markets. Domestic prices of rice are holding firm even in the post Aman rice harvest season presumably because of a much higher price prevailing in India. The monetary policy announced in last July the average inflation target was 6.5 per cent and the policy stance of the Bangladesh Bank keep the inflation to be confined within the target. The overall GDP growth may be from 5.5 per cent to 6.00 per cent at the end of the fiscal year. There is already a turnaround in the economy which must be kept under close observation. Private sector credit is reported to have increased. L/C openings for capital machinery and industrial goods have gone up indicating higher investment. Surplus liquidity since the beginning of the Fiscal year must have been largely used up in private sector and import growth drive by a pickup in output and investment activities from the second quarter of the fiscal 2010. Therefore, liquidity surplus will not end up in speculative uses. With increase in the demand for investment e call money rate that was below 1per cent in July last year is now 4 per cent. The L/C opening for the import of capital machinery increased by 28.04 per cent and 22.3 per cent for industrial raw materials imports. Given robust domestic demand, growing recovery in construction sector activities the overall growth outlook for industrial sector output in fiscal 2009-10 appears quite encouraging. Although Aus rice production was not so good, Aman rice production was better.

The recent rise in the price of rice has acted as a strong incentive spurring farmers to expand acreage of their Boro rice crop. Hopefully, agriculture growth this fiscal year will be as good as last fiscal year.

CHAPTER 12

Focussing Millennium
Development Goals (MDGs)

Responding to World's main development
challenges the Millennium Development
Goals (MDGS) have set eight goals. These goals are
drawn from the actions and targets contained in

the Millennium Declaration that was adopted by 192 United Nations member states, signed by 147 heads of state and Governments and 23 international organizations during the Millennium Summit in September, 2000. These eight MDG goals break down into 21 quantifiable targets and measured indicators as presented are shown in the table below:

Goal 1: Eradicate extreme poverty and hunger
Goal 2: Achieve universal primary education
Goal 3: Promote gender equality and empower women
Goal 4: Reduce child mortality
Goal 5: Improve maternal health
Goal 6: Combat HIV/AIDS, malaria and other diseases
Goal 7: Ensure environmental sustainability
Goal 8: Develop a global partnership for development

Working of MDGs

In a single package MDGs synthesise many of the most important commitments made separately at the international conferences and summits of the 1990s, are as follows:

- Recognize explicitly the interdependence between growth, poverty reduction and sustainable development;
- Acknowledge that development rests on the foundations of democratic governance, the rule of law, respond for human rights, peace and security.

The MDGs are based on time-bound and measurable targets accompanied by indicators for monitoring progress. The MDGs place greater emphasis through the 8th goal the joint responsibilities of developing countries and developed countries as per terms of global partnership endorsed at the International Conference on Financing for Development in Monterrey, Mexico in March, 2002 and again at the Johannesburg World Summit on sustainable Development in August, 2002.

In 2001 UN Secretary General presented the Road Map towards the implementation of the United Nations Millennium Declaration with an integrated and comprehensive overview of the situation. The United Nations further outlines the actions designed to meet the goals and commitments of the Millennium Declaration. Looking ahead to 2015 and beyond there is no question that overreaching goal can be achieved i.e. it is possible to put an end to poverty. The MDGs represent a global partnership that has grown from the commitments and targets established at the world summits of the 1990's. Responding to the world's main development challenges and to the calls of civil society, the MDGs promote poverty reduction, education, maternal health, gender equality, and aim at combating child mortality, AIDS and other diseases.

2015 has, therefore, been set for MDGs goals to be achieved, if all countries of the United Nations work together and do their part to achieve the goals. Poor countries have pledged to govern better and invest in their people through health care and education. Rich countries have pledged to support them through aid, debt relief and fairer trade.

UNDP working with a wide range of partners to help create coalitions for change to support the goals at global, regional and national levels and build the institutional capacity, policies and programs needed to achieve the goals. UNDP's work on and the MDGs focuses on coordinating global and local efforts that campaign and mobilize for the MDGS through advocacy.

REVIEW OF MILLENNIUM DEVELOPMENT GOALS

The Millennium development are eight international development goals that 192 United Nations member states of which 23 are reducing extreme poverty, reducing child mortality rates, fighting disease epidemics, such as, AIDS and developing a global partnership for development.

In 2001, recognizing the need to assist the impoverished nations in aggressive manner the member states of the United Nations adopted the targets.

The MDGs aim to spur development by improving social and economic conditions of the world's poorest countries. The MDGs targets were derived from earlier targets that were officially established at the millennium Summit in 2000 where all leaders present adopted the United Nations Millennium Declaration. These eight goals were particularly promoted from this Declaration.

PROGRESS TOWARDS ACHIEVING THE GOALS

According to the recent report progress towards reaching the goals has been uneven. While some countries have been achieving their goals others are not on track to realize any of the goals. The major countries that have been achieving their goals are China and India. In China poverty population has reduced from 452 million to 278 million. Areas needing the most reduction, such as, the Sub-Saharan Africa regions have yet to make any drastic changes in improving their quality of life. The Sub-Saharan Africa reduced their poverty by about 1per cent and these countries are at major risk not meeting the MDGs by 2015. According to the Overseas Development Institute the fundamental issues will determine whether or not the MDGs are achieved namely the gender, the divide between the humanitarian and development agendas and economic growth.

In order to accelerate progress towards the MDGS the G-8 Finance Ministers met in London in June 2005 and reached an agreement to provide funds to the World Bank, the MF and the African Development Bank (ADB), to cancel an additional $ 40-55 billion in debt by HIPC nations. These funds will enable the impoverished nations to rechannel the resources saved from the foreign debt to social programs for improving health and education and for alleviating poverty.

With the G-8 funding the World Bank, the IMF and the ADB each implemented the Multilateral Debt Relief Initiative (MDRI) to effectuate the debt cancellations. The MDRI supplements HIPC completion point 100 per cent forgiveness of its multilateral debt. However, the countries that previously reached the decision point became eligible, for full debt forgiveness once their lending agency confirmed that the countries had continued to maintain the reforms implemented during HIPS. Other countries that subsequently reach the completion point automatically receive full forgiveness of their multilateral debt under MDRI.

The World Bank and ADB limit MDRI to countries that complete the HIPC program. It has been decided that instead of limiting eligibility to HIPC any country with annual per capita income of $380 or less qualifies for MDRI debt cancellation.

MDGs GOALS

1. Eradicate extreme poverty and hunger

   Halve between 1990 and 2015 the proportion of people whose income is less than a dollar a day. Achieve full and productive employment and decent work for all including women and young people.
   Halve between 1990 and 2015 the proportion of people who suffer from hunger.

2. Achieve universal primary education
   Ensure that by 2015 children everywhere boys and girls alike will be able to complete a full course of primary schooling.

3. Promote gender equality and empower women
   Eliminate gender disparity in primary and secondary education preferably by 2005 and at all levels by 2015.

4. Reduce child mortality
   Reduce by two-thirds between 1990 and 2015 the under-five mortality rate.

5. Improve maternal health
   Reduce by three-quarters between 1990 and 2015 the maternal mortality ratio. Achieve by 2015, universal access to reproductive health.

6. Combat HIV/AID, malaria and other diseases
   Have halted by 2015 and begun to reverse the spread of HIV /AIDS Achieve by 2010 universal

treatment for HIV /AIDS for all those who need it.

Have halted by 2015 and begun to reverse the incidence of malaria and other major diseases.

7. Ensure environmental sustainability

Integrate the principles of sustainable development into country policies and programs and reverse loss of environmental resources. Reduce biodiversity loss by 2010 a significant reduction of loss by 2010. Halve by 2015 the proportion of people without sustainable access to safe drinking water and basic sanitation.

By 2020 to have achieved a significant improvement in the lives of at least 100 million slum dwellers.

8. Develop a global partnership for development

Develop further an open trading and financial system that is rule based, predictable and non-discriminatory. This includes a commitment to good governance, development and poverty reduction nationally and internationally. Address the special needs of the least developed countries that include tariff and quota free access for their exports, enhanced program of debt relief for heavily indebted poor countries. This also includes cancellation of official bilateral debt and more generous official development assistance for countries committed to poverty reduction.

Address the special needs of the land locked and small island developing countries through national and international measures to make debt sustainable in the long term.

In cooperation with pharmaceutical companies provide access to affordable essential drugs in developing countries. And in cooperation with the private sector make available the benefits of new technologies, information and communications.

CHAPTER 13

Global Economic Outlook and Development Challenges in Bangladesh

R ecent economic outlook reveals that the world is consuming more than it produces. This has caused higher prices of food for years to come attributed to expansion of farming for fuel and global climate change and resulted in social unrest almost at unmanageable magnitude particularly in countries already in the grip of severe shortage of food grains. As observed by the International Food Policy Research, bio fuel expansion alone could push maize prices up over two thirds by 2020 and increase oil seed costs by nearly half with subsidies constituting tax on the poorer sections of the society. Global cereal stocks have sunk to their lowest level since the 1980s attributed to reduction of plantings and poor weather. This is reflected in the decline of stock and storage level.

Recent reports indicate that the countries, such as, Mexico have already experienced food riots over soaring prices in the face of declining stock level. If the situation continues unabated exhaustion of stocks is bound to reach and the days of falling prices of food may just be over. Surging demand for food, feed and fuel have recently led to drastic price increases. Climate change is also going to have a negative impact on food production threatening the overall food reserve in poor countries. On the other side, growing financial interest in commodity markets as prices climb is fuelling price volatility in the face of increasing prices of world cereal and energy prices. Already oil prices are hovering around $90 a barrel affecting the countries struggling in their efforts for industrialization and urbanization for higher income growth. More so, for the countries already suffered dramatic impacts from a tripling in wheat prices and near doubling of rice prices since early 2000. What is needed on a priority basis is massive investment in agricultural productivity and technology, a social network much stronger than the existing one, an end to trade barriers, improved infrastructure and financial opportunities in less developed countries that will help improve food security. Although increased trade is a key demand of many developing countries in global talks that would bring economic gains, but in many cases it would not significantly reduce poverty. Stronger view is that global warming can cut worldwide income from agriculture by 16 per cent by 2020 despite potential for increased yields in some colder areas and fertilizing impact on plants of having higher carbon dioxide concentrations in the atmosphere. The increased risk of droughts and floods due to rising temperatures crop yield losses are imminent, Africa would be hit particularly hard by changes in weather patterns in which scientists say manmade gases pumped in to the atmosphere are an important factor. The effects of climate change may bring about threefold increase in the number of undernourished people in Sub-Saharan Africa between 1990 and 2080. Bio fuels also threaten nutrition for the poor. Investment plans assuming expansion in nations with high potential but without detailed plans maize prices would rise a quarter by the end of the next decade. Even prices could climb up to 72 per cent for maize and 44 per cent for oilseeds, it is estimated. Global food demand is shifting towards higher value vegetables, diary, fruits and meat as a result of rapid economic growth in developing countries including China and India. But it can be difficult for smaller farmers to take advantage of large retailers growing grip on the market and their high safety, quality and other requirements.

FOOD PRODUCTION AND CLIMATE CHANGE

Agricultural production across the world has been predicted to be seriously affected by climate change in coming decades. According to a recent research report, progressive climate changes are predicted to rise in temperature from 1 to 5 degree Celsius in coming decades that may put severe blow on food supply. There is a need to account the causes of extreme seasonal rise in temperature, heat, drought or rain and multiple effects of diseases and other ecological upsets that may intensify in future. There are three researches from Europe, North America and Australia including Francesco Tubiello, a physicist and agricultural expert at NASA/ Goddard Institute of Space Studies for the Proceeding of National Academy of Sciences (PNAS). In order to keep pace with population growth, current production of grain from which humans get two thirds of their protein requirement is likely to be doubled and reach to 4 billion tons a year before 2100. These hopes are likely to turn abortive due to decline of agricultural production in the tropical region. The research report says that the developing countries may lose 135 million hectares of prime farm land in the next 50 years in tropical region while increase of temperature rises is expected to start adversely affecting northern crops as well. The temperature may also accelerate outbreaks of weeds and pests and affect plant or animal physiology. Further, higher temperatures may limit the ability of modern dairy cow breeds and lead to decline of livestock fertility and longevity. The temperature rise in the North latitudes would also improve the ability of the crop pests and insects in winters making them strengthen to attack spring crops. The farmers may temporarily mitigate some effects of changing climate by moving toward adaptations that would enable the farmers to switch to different crops or change the timing of plantings and introduction of new varieties or species. But then, such an adaptation plan might require several decades for nations to agree on ways for slowing down or reversing the trend of global warming. The above is a pen picture of situation obtaining globally on the food front and let us have a look on the current development challenges in Bangladesh.

DEVELOPMENT CHALLENGES

At this critical juncture and complex of situations obtaining globally we are having the hardest time in history which calls for work on a firmer and stronger policy frame work on the following:

- Market prices, particularly of food prices need to be stabilized at a lower level based on realistic growth projection;
- Building up a stock level of food grains through internal and external procurement to meet the critical shortage of the deficit areas through a well-designed policy of surplus and deficit areas of food grains within the country;

- Addressing inequality of income growth between the farm and non-farm sector;
- Augmentation of investment in the private sector;
- Higher growth of domestic savings both in rural and urban sectors;
- Expanding domestic tax base through higher income growth in the hitherto neglected sectors;
- Improving quality of ADP implementation;
- Improving investment in agriculture for higher productivity through technological innovations;
- Proper utilization of allocation in power, education and health sectors;
- Sustaining FDI flow;
- Greater mobilization of equity capital;
- Pushing forward structural reforms;
- Greater foreign aid flow;

CHAPTER 14

Fiscal Policy Development in
Tonga - South Pacific

F iscal Policy plays an active role in the development efforts in Tonga - South Pacific. Throughout 1980's the Government pursued not only cautious but also pragmatic fiscal policies with a view to maintaining balance in the recurrent budget. Tax and expenditure measures were, in general, taken in a flexible manner to generate public savings. The development budgets continued to be financed mainly through grant aid and concessionary loans from multilateral financial institutions. The fiscal stance taken by the Government resulted in the accumulation of net positive balances in the banking system. Simultaneously, the private sector had an easy access to domestic credit.

The fiscal system was, thus, reoriented to encourage private savings and investment in the 1980's which provided the necessary impetus towards a sustainable growth pattern in the later period.

Fiscal Measures

In 1986-87 the steep marginal taxes on income were replaced by a flat 10 per cent income tax rate while the corporate tax rate for resident companies was reduced from 25 per cent to 15 per cent. Port & Service taxes were raised from 10 per cent to 15 per cent along with the imposition of sales tax at 5 per cent. In that year the Government granted a 50 per cent increase in wages & salary. This caused a considerable deterioration in the fiscal situation of the Government. In fact, the wage award was intended to remove the disparity that existed between private and public sector wages. Over half of the increase in public sector wages was provided in 1989/90 and the remainder in 1990/91. As a result of the increase in the wage settlement there was an increase of 28 per cent in total recurrent expenditures. Since this increase in expenditure was not accompanied by either new revenue measures or effective reduction in non-productive expenditures Financial Year 1990 ended with a deficit of Tongan $3.7 million in the recurrent budget with an overall deficit of Tongan $34 million (excluding grants) which was 23 per cent of GDP over levels achieved in 1988/89. In 1990/91 budget additional revenue measures were introduced which included increases in taxes on imported beer, tobacco, meats and fuel. At the same time modifications were made in sales tax to bring down administrative costs and improve revenue collection. Alongside, new policies were adopted which worked towards erosion of the tax base. For example, income from farming and fishing were exempted from income tax until June, 1995. Further, although personal income tax was increased Company donations to Charitable Organisations were allowed deductions from corporate tax. While the Port & Service tax was increased exemption from fuel import duties enjoyed by Tonga Electric Power Board was terminated. Despite some restraint in Development expenditures and net lending the overall budget registered a substantial deficit which was 19 per cent of GDP resulting in an increase in net claims on the Government by the banking system. In order to meet the deficit the Government floated a bond of Tongan $4 million out of which Tongan $ 3.4 million was taken by National Reserve Bank of Tonga (NRBT).

1991-92 BUDGET POLICY

Although 1991/92 budget proposed to maintain a balance the proposed development expenditures and net lending were substantially larger than in previous years. No revenue measures were taken in that year. Rather in July 1991imports of Cigarettes for sporting and musical events were exempted from import duties and Port & Service tax. In order to tighten its budgetary stance the Government in May 1992 reduced spending authorisations to the Ministries and Departments and restricted the duty concessions to Sports Clubs. However, due to poor collections of import duties the overall budget showed deficits with the result that the net debtor position of Government increased to Tongan $ 3.4 million by July, 1991. The total fiscal deficit in 1991/92 was nearly 20 per cent of GDP. This was nearly 50 per cent higher than that which was estimated at budget time.

1992-93 BUDGET

The budget for 1992/93 aimed to balance both the recurrent and overall budget. Recourse to domestic borrowing was to be avoided through a contribution from the Tonga Trust Fund. A number of new revenue measures were introduced including an increase in the sales tax on imported motor spirits and diesel, an increase in cigarette duties, higher wharfage and stamp duties and imposition of a 2.5 per cent room tax in hotels for tourists.

REVENUE MOBILISATION

Revenue mobilisation efforts can contribute to the restoration of fiscal balance if fiscal discipline is maintained through:

- a tightening of concessions granted under the development incentive scheme.
- improved effectiveness of collections of revenue from foreign trade taxation.
- improved administrative efficiency to generate a sustained level of income tax collection.
- regular review of Public utility charges.

These steps in fiscal administration besides helping to meet the revenue target improved the buoyancy of the tax system in Tonga. Since Tonga's tax efforts are relatively high compared to other middle income countries any increase in either tax rates or tax base will need to reassess the existing tax measures in the light of their potentiality to generate increased revenue.

The main thrust of fiscal reform needs to be put upon expenditure control the filling up of vacant posts may be slowed and consideration should be given to a freeze on new posts. Thus, in the medium term, size of the civil service needs to be reduced as e the civil service wages constitute more than 50 per cent of the recurrent expenditure including pensions and non-wage emoluments. There is an equally urgent need to address non-wage current spending requirements as well as Incentive Schemes which will encourage public officers to leave and take up alternative activities in the private sector. The establishment of a contributory Pension scheme is another essential policy stance in the expenditure control the benefits of which would be portable and independent of employers. Both the new recruits and the existing employees may join the scheme. The Government may pay lump sums to the scheme equivalent to the present value of future pension liabilities.

In reducing fiscal outlays, containing inflationary pressures, reducing the relative attractiveness of civil service and enhancing the competitiveness of the economy, wage restraint will play an important role. Wages in the Government sector will influence the wage bill in the private sector directly. This has serious consequences in the competitiveness of Tonga's exports. Tonga's wages for both skilled and unskilled are among the highest in the Pacific region. Tonga's rural wage rates are higher which together, with high transport cost is a great barrier to development of competitive markets for exportable goods. A Five year cycle of wage adjustment is followed by the Government. Future wages should not be linked to past inflation; rather this should be linked to future price stability and gradual improvement in productivity.

FOREIGN TRADE TAXATION

A system of tariff and duty controls regulates the external trade in Tonga. Custom duties are levied on an ad valorem basis i.e., CIF value of imports except tobacco products and alcoholic beverages which are levied on a specific basis. The purpose of the tariff structure is to raise revenue although protective duties are levied on items notably beer, paint and wire fencing material.

CUSTOM DUTIES ON MAJOR CATEGORIES OF IMPORTS

1. Ad valorem	Range (percentage of value)
Agricultural products	0-30
Mineral products (other than Petroleum)	0-15
Textiles	15-20
Machinery	0-15
Motor Vehicles	15-45

2. Specific	
Kerosene	0 per litre
Gasoline	35c per litre
Diesel fuel	35c per litre
Beer	200 per cent or T$2.10
Wire	75 per cent or T$3.20 per litre
Spirits	300 per cent or T$20 per litre
Liquors	200 per cent or T$20 per litre.

PORT & SERVICE TAX

20 per cent Port & Service tax is levied on ad valorem basis except the holders of Development Licence. This cost covers costs of port handling and other related costs. Imports of raw materials in the cases of certain classes of investors and imports of semi-finished products used in exports are exempt from the port & service tax. The import of capital goods is eligible for a 50 per cent exemption. In general, the Government policy relating to imports has been guided by considerations of raising revenue.

However, for a small number of products import duties have been used for protecting domestic production of goods. At present, there is a high rate of protective tariff enjoyed by locally produced beer. Since Tonga's domestic market is small in size the scope for import substitution through trade protection is limited.

On the other hand, a continued reliance on high rate of protective tariff is likely to end up with high level of domestic cost structure. This would only generate inflation through further wage pressures and result in diminution of competitive advantage of exports from Tonga. Therefore, any additional protective tariff must take into account possible macro-economic impact as Tonga has a natural benefit of trade protection due to remoteness and high shipment costs.

IMPORTS OF PERSONAL BELONGINGS

Although detailed figures are not available import of personal belongings from fiscal policy point of view is subject to critical review. According to rough approximation 50 per cent of all container arrivals in Tongatapu are exempt from custom duties as these are labelled as personal effects irrespective of what these containers are intended for. As penalties are not imposed these mislabelled containers have been enjoying a free status of personal belongings alongside high import duties on cars, house building materials and consumer goods. This free status has given the Tongans living abroad to send remittances in kind as personal belongings. Customs revenues are as a result below the targeted revenue. The administrative cost of Customs administration also rises.

Those who have to pay the appropriate duties in the formal sector lose market share to duty free curb market. The solution in this case is to maintain a regulatory disincentive to the abuse of the duty-free personal belongings exemption in the customs code.

There is one option i.e., to impose stiff penalties on those found guilty of abusing the duty free provisions. These penalties include confiscation of all mislabelled goods, payment of punitive duty rates and loss of future import privileges. From fiscal policy point of view it is necessary to see that the Government does not have to incur losses on account of the misuse· of duty free provisions. Further, the irregularities in the import of duty free goods on personal belongings that favour informal market activities over formal private sector development need to be removed and corrected through legislative changes.

Changes in Tax Policy

A major tax reform was undertaken by the Government in the mid 1980's reducing income and company tax rates. Customs duties were increased and the range of specific fees and charges increased. Thus, indirect taxes provide an increasingly greater share of Government revenues. Amendments to the IDI Act were made in 1990 extending the scope and the extent of tax incentives to the private sector in the case of approved projects.

Tax rates on income and profits are relatively low. Taxes on individuals are a flat 10 per cent of taxable income with farming and fishing income exempted up to 1995.

Corporate income tax for domestic Companies is 15 per cent on the first Tongan $ 10,000 of taxable profits and 30 per cent for amount in excess of this. In the case of certain groups of non-resident Companies including airlines, insurance and shipping the tax is based on turnover i.e.; 1.25 per cent for airlines and shipping and 2.5 per cent of the premiums paid for insurance Companies.

The Corporate tax for all other foreign Companies is 37.5 per cent on the first Tongan $ 50,000 of net profits and 42.5 per cent on amounts above Tongan $ 50,000. However, for export oriented ventures corporate tax is 17 per cent. The Companies based in Tonga having 80 per cent trade outside Tonga have the lowest tax i.e., 10 per cent including accelerated depreciation and tax credits for exports. In addition, Companies may carry forward losses and can be exempted from the withholding tax. Tax concessions available to approved enterprises under IDIA are a tax holiday period of up to 15 years and a refund of import duty on raw materials and semi-finished products if the final product is exported. The collection of income tax can be postponed until after the expiration of the tax holiday. In November 1992 the IDIA was further amended. Under the revised Act tax holidays are no longer provided for expansion of investment. Loss of carry forward is not allowed nor is depreciation of capital goods after the expiration of the holiday period. Investors eligible for a tax holiday under IDIA were granted full exemption from the port and services taxes. IDIA tax holidays are allowed in the case of the firms which include manufacturers, engineering work shops, tourism facilities, commercial firms and fisheries for export.

The rationality for generous tax incentives is that these may work as strong inducements for private sector investment. Experience has proved that such tax incentives are of only secondary importance in deter mining whether to invest in Tonga or not.

Other factors which are of immediate relevance are the cost of labour, access of labour, access to outside markets and the overall policy framework. The tax holidays may work as incentive for encouraging establishment of inefficient enterprises to erode the fiscal base and distort incentives in favour of those firms or sub-sectors which deserve tax relief.

In phasing out the use of tax holidays as an investment incentive it is necessary to link this with the reduction in corporate tax levels in order to achieve greater and permanent inducement to enterprise activity. Higher corporate tax rates vis-a-vis personal income tax rates serves as a serious disincentive to the formation of modern, corporate forms of enter prise organisation. Tonga's liberal tax holiday provisions apply for the export oriented industries in agriculture and fisheries. These are largely exempted from import duties on capital goods and raw materials and these should remain as a means of ensuring the competitiveness of export oriented industries.

This treatment of providing tax incentives to the export oriented industries in agriculture does not imply that they be exempted from taxes on income and consumption. Taxes on income and consumption should be levied on all classes of consumers including those supplying farm products for export.

The fiscal policy needs to be reoriented in order to generate greater amount of resources through an evolutionary change in the taxation structure and in this "equity" should be the prime objective of the Government. The tax burden should be borne by each sector in proportion to its taxable capacity. The taxation policy should aim at improving the income of the farmers, fishermen, traders, industrials, exporters and then enable them to contribute to the growth of the economy. Non-tax income of the Government is now limited. Its base needs to be increased in the process of the growth of the financial institutions and their profitability and through widening of the investment portfolio of the Government.

CHAPTER 15

Development through Gender equality between men and women worldwide in the perspective of Millennium Development Goals

Development needs to be perceived from the grass-root level of centuries old ideology, traditions of human habits, culture and outlook that grew since time immemorial. Gender equality is an expression of thoughts and modes of policies of the Government and agencies that have shaped the world destiny towards a higher and broader horizon of human advancement. Gender equality is, no doubt, essential for growth and poverty reduction. But unfortunately, Gender inequality is ingrained in our cultural, social behaviour and evolution of the political system and changes in such a way that needs an overhauling of the whole system for a well-coordinated development policies and programs for uplifting of the sense of societal values. What has been the thinking and strategic position of this vital aspect of human development and efforts to establish this as human right in the world agenda of growth strategy in the present day world is the theme of this paper.

Domestic policy action plays a crucial role in gender equality and that needs to be supplemented by the policy action taken on the international front by the joint efforts of world community through collection of evidence based data and evaluation of the impact. Before proceeding further on this subject it would be appropriate to emphasize the main facets and messages of the World Development Report of 2012.

Gender equality needs to be looked as it can enhance gains in productivity and outcomes in terms of output that automatically benefit and rollover generation to generation making institutions equally representative by men and women. According to a recent World Development Report 2012, women represent 40 per cent of the total global labor force and 43 per cent of the total agricultural force and more than half of the world's university students. Gains in productivity through development of skills and talents are usually through equal access of women and men to agricultural and other inputs for raising yields and labor productivity.

In Malawi and Ghana, for example. an increase of control over household resources by women have brought about growth prospects mainly through changing spending patterns that benefit to a greater extent women's' education and health. In countries, such as, Brazil, Nepal, Pakistan and Senegal, women decision making process through empowerment of women in economic and many socio-political activities and movement for establishing viable democratic society both at local and urban society level for better and quality provision of goods and services. Global and national development through gender equality has brought about perceptible decline in many disadvantages faced by women and girls over the last three decades. These are rooted and visible at the policy level particularly in areas, such as, educational enrolment, life expectancy and labor force participation.

As a result of Government initiatives in countries particularly Latin America, the Caribbean and the East Asia gender gaps are closing noticeably in respect of educational enrolment while in other developing countries girls are coming forward and often outnumber the boys in enrolment in both secondary schools and universities.

There are factors other than income growth that have worked to deliver increased gender equality mainly through reorganization and reforms of markets and institutions both formal and informal interacting household decisions in favor of educating girls and young women. Income growth through opening of new markets have caused new employment opportunities for women and formal institutions by expanding schools and lowering costs which have acted favorably influencing household decisions for sending girls and young women to formal educational institutions in many developing countries.

In spite of this positive growth of gender equality, gender disparities or gaps are still wide: such as, excess deaths of girls and women, disparities in girls' schooling, unequal access to a wide variety of economic opportunities apart from differences in voice in households and in society still exist. Gender gaps exist where poor women living in poor places are confronted with disadvantages, such as remoteness, ethnicity and other forms of disability. Child births often occur almost without parental care. This situation of gender gaps is often aggravated by other norms of societal behaviour or mal practices rampant in the exercise of rights of ownership and control over land and other assets amid functioning of modern markets and formal institutions which disfavor women and keep them in a greater distance.

The above is a vivid picture of gender gaps that exists and needs to be addressed on the global front through openness of trade and exchange of information and communication technologies that have the potential of putting a brake in the growth of inequality between men and women through establishing a connectivity of women with the wheels of modern markets and technologies and capturing economic opportunities for which declared public policy decision and action should simultaneously work for promoting gender equality in all spheres of life. The priorities for public policy makers in order to close or gradually reduce the gender equity gaps will need to reorient policies on the domestic front that will result in reaping the greatest benefit to the society instead of attacking the issue with only higher incomes strategy.

The World Development Report - 2012 sets forth the priorities distinctly as follows:

- Addressing excess deaths of girls and women and eliminating gender disadvantage in education where these have established firmly
- closing differences in access to economic opportunities and the ensuing earnings and productivity gaps

- Shrinking gender differences in voice within households and societies and limiting the reproduction of gender inequality from generation to generation.

While focused and sustained domestic public prescription is all the more important the inherent causes of gender gaps need to be investigated and brought to the floor for action by the Government agencies. In cases of maternal mortality and differential access to economic opportunities multiple actions will need to be initiated to deal with various impediments that hinder the process of bringing about equality in gender gaps. Other impediments limiting the progress will need to be addressed to prioritize are:

- reduce excess deaths of girls and women
- shrinking persistent educational gaps
- narrow down disparities between women and men in earnings and productivity
- diminishing gender differences in household and societal voice

The international community's role in the priority areas are generally through supporting evidenced based public action with the aid of improved data collection and evaluation of impact in priority areas In some priority areas adjustment of current support ensuring that the education for all reaches the disadvantaged girls and boys. In some other areas it will demand new and additional action on multiple fronts –a combination of more funding with coordinated efforts to foster innovation and learning and effective partnerships. These actions should be directed in supporting the poorest countries in reducing excess deaths of girls and women through greater investment supplying clean water, sanitation and maternity services and removing persistent gender gaps in education sector. Increased and continued support is needed to improve the gender disaggregated data in order to carry out more experimentation and systematic evaluation of mechanism to improve the access of women to modern established markets and delivery of services. In all these actions the partnerships beyond Governments should include the private sector, civil society organizations and academic institutions in both developing and advanced countries.

Gender equality is at the root of development. Its evolution in recent decades has changed for the better even though women are still struggling with many disadvantages and disfavour in their living standard and status. In a general observation in the developed and developing countries women have gained many advantages and facilities in the exercise of their rights in education, health care, access in technical and non-technical jobs for earnings for their livelihoods which was unthinkable for women living in remote villages only in the recent past. Now-a-days many African countries, the Pacific, South Asia and Caribbean countries have extended equal rights under the law in such aspects of human resource development as property ownership, inheritance as well as marriage laws as fundamental human rights.

The World Development Report has mentioned about guaranteeing equality of all citizens in the constitutions of 136 countries. Whatever the progress in this area has been achieved but it has not been uniform in all aspects of gender equality in all countries. For example, women dying during child birth in Sub-Saharan Africa and in South Asia in the present century are almost of the same trend as it was in Northern Europe in the n the 19ᵗʰ century. The pattern of gender inequality between rich families and poor families indicate that in case of boy or girl the average years of schooling is around 10 years in case of richer group of families than the poorer group whose average years are often lower than six months. This differential pattern of schooling has caused women to die relative to men in the richer group. However, the rate of mortality is high in low and middle income countries relative to high income countries. Besides, divorce or early widow-hood causes many young women to become landless often losing their own earned and inherited assets. This is the gravity of the situation in the poor countries often compelling poor women to cluster in sectors and occupations characterized as women with lower paying.

Above all these, the economically deprived women become victims of the cruel attitude of the higher middle class with many kinds of violence at home with severe physical injuries of women in managing household affairs. There is no escape from this situation as almost everywhere representation of women in political or other local varied organizations is either absent or negligible to address the problem. The pattern of gender inequality in human and physical capital endowments, physical assets and economic opportunities have been a key feature of on-going development process in many developing countries. Gender equality is fundamental to human requirement for living in comfortable and care free conditions whether one is a man or women. He or she must be free from deprivation of all the amenities of life that are enjoyed generally by men and women in advanced societies. With the gradual improvement of the conditions surrounding deprivation and neglect of the people living at the lower end of income level gender equality generates high level of economic efficiency and productive capacity to achieve the development goals through effective utilization of human resources.

As propounded by world renowned Economist Amartya Sen – development is a process of expanding freedoms equally for all people implying that gender equality is an inherent and ultimate objective to reach for achieving human welfare in the process of development of a country. With better access to justice and having less income poverty and minimal gaps in well-being between males and females is the goal embodied in Millennium Development Goals 3 and 5 with widespread ratification of the convention on the Elimination of All Forms of Discrimination against Women (CEDAW). The convention as adopted by the United Nations General Assembly has established a comprehensive framework for the advancement of women ratified by 187 countries.

Gender equality is an instrument for development through enhancement of economic efficiency and removing all kinds of barriers preventing women having access to education, opportunities and inputs like men for large productivity gains in present day globalised world. Further, improving women's absolute and relative status feeds many other development outcomes including those for their children.

Another aspect of gender equality is where men and women have equal chances to become socially and politically active, and thus in making and shaping policies for a more representative and socially oriented democratic institutions. This would then lead a country to a firmer and stronger development path.

Development experience in recent times has proved that women's skills and inherent and inherited talents have substantial impact on productivity gains in the poor countries that are struggling for higher standard of living through raising per capita income. This is a trend more exemplified by recent statistics showing more than 40 per cent of the global labor force, 43 per cent of the agricultural labor force and more than half of the world's university students are women.

The most unfortunate and deteriorating part of the situation is that the women generally fail to function to their utmost capability and ingenuity when their spirit of laborious work is untrusted or grossly misdirected, they face utter disregard, humiliation and discrimination in markets and many societal institutions or organizations resulting in rising costs with manifold economic losses to a country. Women farmers are generally deprived of the security of land tenure in many countries especially as in most of the regions in Africa with the result that they have lower access to credit and other agricultural inputs needed to reverse the trend of inefficient land use and lower yields. This discrimination in the supply of credit together with other gender inequalities in access to other productive inputs make it more difficult for female –headed firms to be as productive and profitable as male –headed firms. This is the most unfortunate facet of gender inequality affecting the vast mass of women population in developing poor countries hindering the process of development economics to work in ameliorating the depressed conditions in which women are subject to injustice and inhuman treatment in the society everywhere.

It is estimated by the Food and Agricultural Organization (FAO) that an equal treatment of men and women in the access to productive resources would increase agricultural output by 4 per cent and eliminating barriers preventing women from working in productive sectors or occupations will yield the same results by lowering the productivity gap and increasing output per worker substantially higher than the current level across a number of countries. However, as the countries develop the productivity gains may be even larger in a globalised world where efficiency in the deployment of resources is aimed at achieving a country's competitiveness and growth. Research and investigation indicate that gender inequality has become more cost effective in a world of free trade diminishing a country's ability to compete in international markets. This is particularly true in industries that need equal treatment of men and women for better management and growth.

In countries with rapidly aging population as in China, Europe and Central America, encouraging women to enter and remain in the labor force can help dampen the adverse impact of shrinking working age population. Thus, in globalised world markets gender based inequalities or equalities in countries will have different impacts depending on situation. With this general observation, it may be concluded that Women's endowments, agencies and opportunities can shape the development of gender equality between men and women of next generation. Increasing the share of household resources or income controlled by women generally bring about favorable impact on economic growth. This is corroborated by the fact that increasing the share of household income in countries, such as, Bangladesh, Brazil, Mexico and the United Kingdom, controlled by women either through their own earnings or cash transfers changes spending pattern of women in a way that directly benefit children health by increasing nutritional standards. In China and India, for example, increasing adult female income has a positive effect on surviving girls and years of schooling for both boys and girls. The differences of the impact of female income on the children, however, vary from country to country depending on cultural and educational standards including health of both men and women.

There are differences between men's and women's ability to make choices and transform them into desired actions and outcomes across all countries and cultures. These gender differences often go against the welfare of the women affecting the society in general influencing their ability to build their human capital to take up economic opportunities. With greater control over health and household purchases the women have higher role in providing nutritional foods to all the members of a family in proportion to the nutritional requirement and nutritional standards and status of women.

Women's collective agency can be transformative for society that can shape the institutions, markets and social norms limiting their individual agency and opportunities and empowering women as political and social actors to change policy choices and make institutions more representatives for a range of voices. In the United States, for example, female suffrage led policy makers to turn their attention to child and maternal health helping infant mortality by 8 to 15 per cent. In India, what is observed is that giving power to women at the local level through political quotas led to increases in the provision of public goods and reducing corruption. Villages with female leader in any kind of social or humanitarian work are done generally without bribes which are a common practice in the community in the leadership of men in the developing countries. Greater public voice by women, besides benefiting women and children benefit largely the men in the community. In the advanced countries the economic activities or in implementation of development projects the participation of women in political leadership reshapes social views on balancing work and family life in general. In the opposite situation, men and women, not having equal treatment or chances to be active socially and politically, to influence laws, politics, constitutional policy making process of institutions become more inclined to favor the more influential people and the institutions resulting in greater multiple inequality creeping in the society. In the process, generations of women become automatically deprived of basic education and amenities of civil society to live as equal partners with men to make choices to deploy their potential as human resource.

The conceptual aspect of gender equality refers to the social, behavioral norms determining how a man and woman relate to each other and the consequent differences in the exercise of power between them, while the key dimensions of gender equality are accumulation of endowments - education, health and physical assets and the use of these endowments to take up economic opportunities for gainful employment through investment and reinvestment and generate incomes that can affect their wellbeing in the society and within household.

The World Bank has continued to focus on gender equity and development during the past few decades concentrating their analysis on women's and girls' education as panacea for all round development internally and externally. The unfortunate part of the story is that too many women are still dying in child birth – either they are dying in alarming rate or not born at all. Lack of voice of the women in the household and their inability to participate in decision making process along with civil society members for finding out economic opportunities for them are serious constraints in their free movement with the main stream society. The inequality between men and women is a serious hindrance and it is a stumbling block in the way of mounting efforts in all corners of the globe to curb poverty reduction thereby limiting economic and social development. Real competitiveness and equity are long term sources of economic strength in the worldwide campaign of human resources development through gender equity. As an international financial development bank, the World Bank promotes gender equality mainly through lending and grants to the developing poor countries through their working knowledge and analytical tools. According to recent statistics during FY 2006 - FY 2010 more than $65 billion or 37 per cent of the World Bank's lending and grants were allocated to gender equality operations particularly in education, health, access to land, financial and agricultural services, jobs and infrastructure. As a member of the World Bank group, the International Finance Corporation (IFC) complements the World Bank's work with Governments by supporting the participation of women in business. IFC is working with the private sector in ways that empower women that is good for both business and development.

Investment and advisory services have been developed to increase women's access to finance and access to markets for women entrepreneurs, reduce gender-based barriers in the business environment and create business opportunities built around improved working conditions for women employees. IFC has successfully partnered with financial institutions to reach the women's market including the provision of capacity building to women entrepreneurs and increased access to finance. As a result of this expansion IFC now aims at ensuring by 2013, 25 per cent of the small and medium enterprises receive IFC loans through financial intermediaries are women.

In absolute terms, the World Bank assistance for contributing to gender equity in the poor developing countries may be evaluated as below:

- In developing countries, gender equity has risen from 91 girls for every 100 boys enrolled in primary school and 88girls for every 100 boys enrolled in secondary school ten years ago to 96 girls for every 100 boys enrolled in primary school and 95 girls enrolled in secondary schools now.

- Female life expectancy has increased by 20 to 25 years in most places in the past 50 years, to reach 71 globally.

- Maternal deaths fell from 546, 000 in 1990 to 358000 in 2008. As 99 per cent of these deaths or 355,000 of these deaths still occur in developing countries, the World Bank is redoubling its efforts on reproductive health. The lives of thousands of adolescent girls and young women are improving through job skills and training funded by the Adolescent Girls Initiative and this includes Afghanistan, Haiti, Lao Peoples' Democratic Republic, Jordan, Liberia, Nepal, Rwanda and South Sudan. Thousands of women are having access to credit to finance their small and medium enterprises in many developing countries, such as Tanzania.

- In many countries more and more women are getting land titles and certificates as in Ethiopia. These land titles and certificates have increased the capacity of women to increase productivity of land and apply for further funding to bigger financial institutions for the expansion of their enterprises.

RESULTS ACHIEVED OF WORLD BANK GENDER ACTION PLAN

Results achieved in the field of education in countries like India, Bangladesh and Yemen indicates a substantially promising trend. In India, the IDA financed Elementary Education project has helped the Government enrol nearly 20 million out of school children in elementary school as a result of which India is now close to achieving gender parity in primary education and by 2009, 94 girls were enrolled for every 100 boys in primary school compared to 90 in the early 2000. This trend in primary education is narrowing down the widening gap between boys and girls so much so that the primary education in India is projected to reach parity in gender equality by 2013.

The situation in Bangladesh in the Female Secondary School Assistance Program (1993) financed by IDA supported a Government program to improve access to secondary education for girls by providing tuition stipends that resulted in increasing Girls' enrolment in secondary schools to 3.9 million in 2005 from 1.1 million in 1991 indicating a substantial number from disadvantaged in hitherto neglected and remote areas in Bangladesh. This is an encouraging trend for achieving Bangladesh's Millennium Development Goals in Gender parity in education well ahead of time.

In health sector in Ghana, health insurance coverage has been extended to people extended to people employed in the informal and rural sectors since the inception of the World Bank's financed National Health Insurance Program. Of the insured, 70 per cent are children and pregnant women are exempt from paying premiums. In 2009, 90 per cent of pregnant women use Antenatal care services while births attended by skilled health staff rose from 40 per cent in 2008 to 59 per cent in 2009.

In Afghanistan Health Sector Emergency Reconstruction and Development Project helped millions of people in rural areas access primary health care for the first time. Health care for expectant mothers expanded with the number of deliveries assisted in facility by trained health workers jumping from 6 per cent to 23 per cent and the number of pregnant women who received at least one parental care visit rose from 8,500 in 2003 to 188,670 in 2008. Around 20,000 community health workers –half of them are women, have been trained and deployed throughout the country, increasing access to family planning and boosting childhood vaccinations.

In income and employment sector in Turkey, for example, in a jointly conducted study reveals the factors underlying low female employment, the benefits of getting more women to work with policy priorities for creating increased number of job opportunities for women folk. The study has contributed to mainstreaming female employment and its policies and programs for open public discussion in February 2011 giving incentives to employers for hiring women and introducing separate incentives for self- employed and part time female workers.

The World Bank funded a Gender Equity Model in the National Institute for women in Mexico to promote equal opportunities for men and women which helped overcome cultural barriers in business practices. 300 Mexican organizations by December 2010 were certified as gender equitable while an average of 663 firms per annum continue to be in line to adopt the program in their line operations. The participating firms in the program have been successful in eliminating widespread pregnancy discrimination from recruitment process thereby improving the workers' performance and productivity substantially about noticeable changes in the development of small and medium industries through channelling US $ 500,000 to local micro finance service providers to extend loans to women and provided technical assistance to women clients.

In Tanzania the Gender Action Plan supported an IFC woman targeted project increasing women's access to finance small and medium industries opened up further employment opportunities for women having good repayment records. In Rural Development and Infrastructure Sector in countries, such as, Haiti, India and Vietnam the Gender Action Plan has made substantial progress aiming to focus on equipping women with technical and financial skills to increase crop yields, access markets and increase their incomes improving livelihoods of the rural poor and disadvantaged women. In Haiti, Women Agricultural Producers' Project funded by the Gender Action Plan (GAP) aiming to focus policy on equipping women with both technical and financial skills to increase crop yields and increase income through access to markets. This has facilitated the women producers to work on assessment of their needs of capacity building and to monitor implementation of Gender action plan in the agricultural sector.

In India, Andhra Pradesh District Poverty Initiatives Project and the Andhra Pradesh Rural Poverty Reduction Project was initiated with a view to improve the livelihoods and the quality of life of the rural poor and to withstand the vulnerability of economic and financial shocks. The projects initiated have facilitated small group organization and self-management within rural communities with particular focus on women As reported, nearly 8 million poor women in rural areas have been organized into 629,870 self-help groups and 28,282 village organizations resulting in an increase of incomes by 90 per cent of which 8 million are women.

In Vietnam, World Bank Project financing has been provided to support ethnic minority women to undertake road maintenance in rural areas increasing poor and vulnerable women's employment in remote areas with a view to developing cost effective maintenance of roads. The project has resulted in maintenance of rural roads of around 13,470 Km thereby provided training to 1,533 ethnic minority women from four communes as rural transportation managers. As after effects of the project women of rural areas have achieved greater voice in decision making process in managing affairs at local and household level emanating from increased economic power and social status.

Although Women's participation and empowerment in development activities is one of the major Millennium Development goals and policy initiative, however discussions and debates in this field in world forums have so far been not to the extent expected so that there have been minimal discussions in order to arrive at practical methods of implementation. In reality projects centering women mainly micro credit and cooperatives although create new assets, but often fail to address control of existing resources creating problems in financial mismanagement in many developing countries.

As follow up to the World Conference on women and in the twenty-third special session of the General Assembly of the United Nations – entitled Women 2000 -gender equality, development and peace for the twenty first century emerging issues, trends and new approaches to issues affecting the situation of women in regard to the equality of women and men were discussed. The relevance of gender equality and women's empowerment for sustainable development has long been established in inter-Governmental commitments, such as, the Rio Declaration on environment and Development (Reference: Report of the United Nations Conference on Environment and Development, Rio de Janeiro, 3-14 June, 1992). The Conference presents an unprecedented opportunity to assess the progress in the implementation of international agreements in the context of sustainable development and identify gaps and renew commitments to action in gender responsive sustainable development processes, institutional frameworks and finance mechanisms and women's participation at all levels of decision making process wherein human rights based approach can assist in the elimination of all discriminations against women.

Any convention on gender equity provides the needed framework to hold the states parties accountable for progress on this vital issue of human resources development. After an evaluation of gender equality issues nationally and internationally the basic truth that emanates is that participation, decision making and management roles of women are critical to development on a sustainable path at local, international levels where women can prove as effective agents of change. In the developed countries it is observed that the women are pursuing life styles and consumption patterns that have a greater sense of responsibility towards achieving sustainable development. Women need to come more and more in the public front giving them the opportunities in the discourse on economic development, social progress and environmental protection and management. It is proved in the overall assessment that the companies in the private sector with a stronger representation of women at top management level perform best. This suggests that increase in women's leadership and in decision making positions are helpful in generating an overall capacity of manpower in sustainable development. But Women's lack of or limited access to resources, land, clean water and cheap energy hinders their full participation and often puts them at greater risks at times of natural disasters for which women's platforms have proved to be useful forums at national and international levels for establishing linkage with Governments or other agencies to redress their demands.

As women's access to education, training and capacity development are the main sources for their empowerment and improved livelihoods measures or the policy directions need to be taken sector wise so that there is a greater and closer integration with the movement of economic variables in order to evaluate the real impact of gender equality through targeted public support for equal opportunities for women and girls in areas, such as, education and training, in science and technology.

For a closer link and collaboration, the Governments of countries of both developed and developing countries will need to jointly sit with the academic institutions and education boards, agencies and members of the civil society to redesign educational curricula and teaching materials in order to address the problems of environment and challenges posed by climate change on men and women who are directly or indirectly affected and their differential impact on them generating further inequality in the society. In this disparity, while vocational training can help ensure improved and updated technical knowledge and information, these skills and technical knowledge gained would help contribute towards enhancing women's opportunities for gainful employment for decent and improved living conditions. Herein lies the opportunities for micro-finance to develop and help empowerment of women.

A conscious and well-designed micro finance system as it can be introduced and implemented with measurable targets at the poor community level should be accorded a top priority in the gender equality agenda worldwide. This will obviously need a dedicated spirit and enthusiasm by politicians, social scientists and members of civil society to agree on the principles of its operation and monitor its effective operation for socio-economic upliftment of the people at the lower end of income level. Approximately, 1.6 billion people live without any access to electricity, energy in rural areas –this is a major challenge in our struggle for the improvement of living conditions of people rather to wipe out pockets of poverty in the Pacific and Southeast Asia regions and around the world. The reality of the situation is that an estimated more than 3 billion people are compelled to rely on open fires and traditional cooking stoves utilizing biofuels with the responsibility of collecting firewood falling on women and children. They often take several hours to collect firewood from distant places from their homes to hilly areas in jungles spending several hours and this is indeed arduous jobs only to fulfil their consumption needs of energy. The time spent on this would have been invested in profitable ventures for enhancement of the capacity of rural women to pursue education and income generating activities like those of the urban women, thus fulfilling the targets set for achievement of

Millennium Development Goals and facing the adverse effects of climate change.

Solar power has increasingly been used in both developed and developing countries to power homes, schools and health centres besides providing access to information and communication technology. Besides, solar-powered pumping systems have helped increase agricultural output in women's collectives allowing them to grow their business and enhance food security and women's economic empowerment. Effective and safe waste management is another challenge in both developed and developing countries. It has been estimated that globally 20 million people earn their living from collecting solid waste within the informal sector. However, efforts have been made to formalize this sector by providing waste pickers with social safety nets and access to credit, training and education in recycling management. Where waste materials remain uncollected in slums and poor neighbourhoods, men and women have equally accepted a challenge for the collection of waste into income generating opportunities. Besides, there are many Women's community based initiatives in many countries. If these community initiatives or community based enterprises are integrated in a common platform with the multi-sectoral national planning and the budgetary policy framework and management, these will then go a long way in promoting sustainable development through establishing gender equality. Many countries are having a variety of institutional mechanisms, legislative provisions, policies and programs to promote gender equality linked with economic development. However, in all these development works the key challenges are mutual understanding of the Government and private agencies on the need and importance of women's participation in the green activities of the economy. What is needed in establishing gender equality in the development efforts is to tackle the vested interests in the key areas of the economy especially the environmental and service related sectors to step up efforts to promote gender equality and sustainable development.

Above all, what is required is a strong will and consensus among the political leaders for well managed governance and this is a key factor for a revolutionary change in the social system to bring about gender parity. Its ongoing implementation and success depend on how the Government takes initiative in adopting and implementing economic, social, social framework, policies and programs with civil society and the private sector and the donor agencies as important partners.

The Council of the European Union supporting the achievement of the Millennium Development Goals by 2015 has already put forward a Twelve point Action Plan for implementation of necessary policy change to take concrete actions and calls for collective action by all stakeholders which will have salutary effects on the developing countries growth prospects. Although there has been notable progress in the countries of the European regions on MDGs – but progress has been uneven and considerable work needs to be done in the region's most lagging behind especially in Sub-Saharan Africa and the least developed countries drawing special attention to the countries in situations of conflict and fragility. What is required in the progress is quality and coherence of the work of development partners. Since MDGs are mutually interlinked, mutually dependent and reinforcing a holistic and rights based approach taking into account local conditions and context is required in the present situation.

An interdependence of the MDGs with human rights, gender equality, democracy, good governance, development, peace and security, climate and energy as well as non-development policies for achieving the MDGs need to be reconciled for fruitful results. Inclusive finance and effective social protection systems as well as reducing inequality are essential for each developing country to achieve the MDGs. The role of the private sector is crucial –its impact will be large in terms of employment and income generation.

MDGs have mobilising role for development on a global level and then this should be translated in the local level. The EU calls on them to reinforce their ownership and leadership by incorporating the MDGs into national development strategies for which democratic governance is central element. Other factors are transparency and accountability to all citizens in all countries at all levels, all stakeholders –central and local Governments, civil society organizations and the private sector for progress on development outcomes.

The EU calls upon all parties in the international community for meaningful and strong partnerships with all stake holders. This includes civil society organizations and social partners, the private sector, multilateral organizations and other actors at all levels. Special emphasis is laid on the most vulnerable and excluded –the poor and the hungry people with disabilities at the centre of development with special focus on women for their participation and empowerment.

Recognizing the interdependence of progress on the different MDGs and the impact of off-track MDGs, such as, hunger, child and maternal health and sanitation, on the achievement of progress in other areas the European Council puts emphasis on EU policy framework to assist developing countries in addressing food security challenges and on the EU role in Global Health essential to the achievement of MDGs. The EU reiterates its strong commitment to gender equality as human right and a question of social justice in EU development policy. Keeping in view the Gender equality as the goal in achieving MDGs, the European Council has adopted the EU plan of Action on Gender equality and Women's Empowerment in Development 2010-2015.

Gender equality, women's political and economic empowerment and women's enjoyment of human rights are essential for poverty reduction and sustainable development for women as economic actors and for addressing the main health challenges with particular links to nutrition, water and sanitation and maternal mortality. The EU supports the establishment of composite UN Entity for Gender equality and the Empowerment of Women. In this the member states of the EU will enhance their support for their education plans in order to enable them to improve their access to quality education for all children irrespective of their background, ethnicity, gender, disability, health, home language and socio-economic status. The EU members are pledged to support this program through bilateral and multilateral channels including through the 'Education for All Fast Track Initiative'.

While designing cultural development programs and strategies the EU encourages partner countries to formulate their cultural policies as an area for international cooperation. The EU also recognizes that natural disasters a serious threat to development and considers a strategy for supporting developing countries in Disaster Risk Reduction as a means of achieving the MDGs.

Furthermore recognizing the importance on Policy Coherence for Development in non-development policies affecting developing countries the EU is committed to support them in achieving the MDGs through its wider political agenda. The Policy Coherence for Development directed for meeting the MDGs in trade and finance, climate change, food security, migration and security. The Council of the European Union encourages the member states for early use of the PCD Work program as a tool to guide EU decision that affect developing countries beyond development. The EU considers that all available financing for development contributes to inclusive and sustainable economic growth that generates decent employment for

achieving MDGs goals. Mobilisation of domestic resources are crucial and central for redistribution of
wealth and for accountability of Governments towards
the citizens and in this fair, effective tax systems and
removing harmful tax practices and evasion will increase domestic resources. With International cooperation and transparency the EU will support developing
countries in building their capacities and will push for
a friendlier international framework promoting good
governance in tax matters.

Regional integration and trade are crucial for significant development benefits, growth and jobs for generating resources to sustain progress towards the MDGs.
The EU is committed to work towards an ambitious,
comprehensive outcome of Doha Development Agenda
containing elements of real value for the poorest in
the developing countries through bilateral and regional trade agreements taking into account their different
needs and development situations. The Council values the potential of WTO compatible with Economic
Partnership Agreements with MDGs. In 2005 in WTO
Hong Kong Ministerial Declaration the EU has made

commitment to provide duty free and quota free market access for all products from all LDCs and calls on other developed countries and the emerging economies to fulfil this commitment to open up their markets for LDC markets. In this connection the EU and the member states have agreed to spend EU $ 2 billion on trade related assistance while their total aid for trade has reached record levels of EU $ 10.4 billion. The EU and its member states agree that a vibrant private sector is dependent on business environment to attract both domestic and foreign investment.

The EU and its member states have agreed to increase their efforts to mobilize the private sector and engage with business activities to accelerate the progress of MDGs by promoting the UN Global Compact and the Corporate Social Responsibility principles.

As a global focal point the EU accounting for more than half of the global ODA reaffirms its commitment to increasing its aid to reach 0.7 per cent of

GNI by 2015. All other international donors are urged to increase their level of spending and contribute to their share to the development efforts. In this connection it is worth mentioning the EU Action Plan 2010-2015 for Gender Equality and Women's Empowerment submitted to the High level meeting of the UN in New York in September 2010 as essential guidance for the whole of EU in support of the MDGs by 2015.

These Action Plans designed to achieve the following objectives are shown in the table below:

Strengthen the lead role of the EU in promoting GEWE in development
Ensure adequate human and financial resources for GEWE - a, Financial resources and b. Build in-house capacity on gender equality issues in development
Place gender equality issues systematically on the agenda of dialogue with partner countries

Ensure that gender equality is mainstreamed in EU funded projects and that general budget and sector budget support programmes use sex-disaggregated indicators and include at least one gender equality performance indicator where relevant prioritise in country actors participation and capacity building and advocacy on GEWE

Improve the EU monitoring, accountability and transparency on allocation of funds for GEWE

Strengthen EU support to partner countries in their efforts to achieve MDGs, in particular MDGs-3 and MDGs - 5

Strengthen EU support to partner countries in combating gender-based violence and all forms discrimination against women and girls.

These objectives will serve as model for implementation of the European Union's activities as a whole not only for the European regions but also for other developed and developing countries' move towards gender equality worldwide in the coming decades.

BIBLIOGRAPHY

Fiscal policy Stabilization, and Growth in Developing Countries, IMF 1989.

Investing in development lessons of World Bank experience, Warren C Banu and Stocks M. Tolbert - Published for the World Bank, 1985.

Asian Development Report - 1996.

UNDP Selected Report On Poverty Alleviation Efforts

Pacific Island Countries: Economic Performance and Selected Issues in Policy Management and Adjustments, United Nations - 1993.

www.ingramcontent.com/pod-product-compliance
Lightning Source LLC
Chambersburg PA
CBHW072302200526
45168CB00014B/162